A-LEVEL

entury
story

ck Murphy

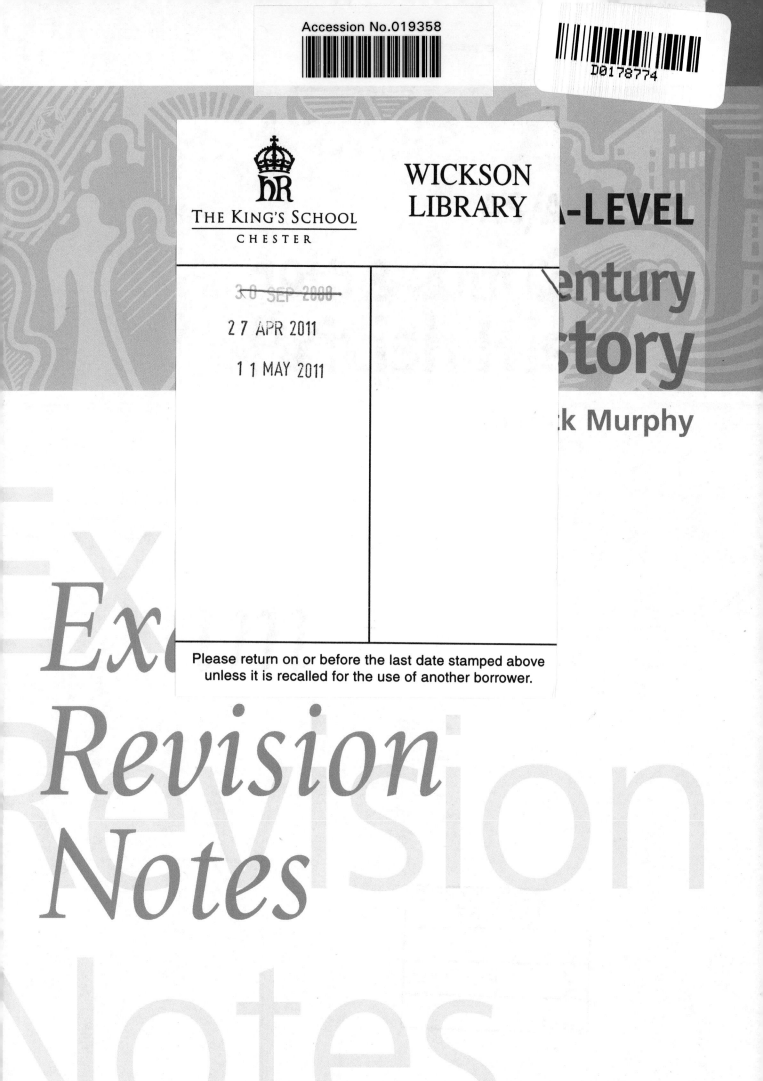

Exc
Revision
Notes

Philip Allan Updates
Market Place
Deddington
Oxfordshire
OX15 0SE

tel: 01869 338652
fax: 01869 337590
e-mail: sales@philipallan.co.uk
www.philipallan.co.uk

ISBN 0 86003 434 8

Cover illustration by John Spencer
Typeset by Magnet Harlequin, Oxford
Printed by Raithby, Lawrence & Co Ltd, Leicester

Contents

Unit 5   Chartism

Unit 6   The era of Gladstone and Disraeli — Liberals and Conservatives, 1846–94

Unit 7   Ireland, 1798–1998

Unit 8   The era of Salisbury and Chamberlain, 1885–1906

Unit 9   Foreign policy, 1890–1914

Unit 10 The Liberal governments, 1905–15

Unit 11 The rise of the Labour Party, 1890–1931

Unit 12 The decline of the Liberal Party, 1914–31

Unit 13 Political and economic history, 1918–39

Unit 14 Foreign policy, 1918–39

Unit 15 Britain in the Second World War, 1939–45

Unit 16 The Labour Party, 1945–97

Unit 17 The Conservative Party, 1945–97

Introduction

About this book

Before you read this book, you should already have read the recommended textbooks, made detailed notes and produced answers to examination questions. These revision notes comprise three important elements:

- **The main factual material** — this is organised in a way which will be easy to remember and revise from.
- **Glossaries of essential terms** — words which are explained in the glossaries are italicised in the text. Make sure you learn and understand these terms.
- **Examiner tips** — these offer advice about what to expect in examinations and how to use the factual material contained in the book.

About the AS and A2 examinations

These notes cover the major AS and A2 modules of the three main examination boards: AQA, Edexcel and OCR. Check with your teacher to find out which examination board specification you are studying. Also check which units you will be examined on.

From the specification which you are studying you should find out the format the examination will take. Some modules/units require you to answer several questions based on **source material**. You might, for example, have to compare material from several sources, or assess the reliability, usefulness or value of a source to a historian, or explain why different historical interpretations appear in different sources.

Other modules/units require you to **explain a historical term** within the context of the topic you have studied. Most examination papers will require you to engage in **extended writing**. This could be a question based solely on your own knowledge. Other questions require you to combine source material and your own knowledge to produce an analytical answer.

Finally, you may have to **write an essay** based on your own knowledge. In AQA AS module 3 you will be required to write a course essay. You will be given the title beforehand but you will have to write the answer under examination conditions using your own notes.

The Advanced Subsidiary (AS) is a new examination. Its standard is meant to be between GCSE and A-level. You might be asked questions which require you to explain causation, e.g. 'Why did...occur?' You might also have to explain the degree of success or the main problems facing a politician or government.

The A2 examination is of GCE A-level standard, requiring you to write balanced, analytical answers by evaluating evidence.

The AS and A2 examinations have some important new features.

- They all require you to demonstrate **knowledge and understanding** of history. This book of revision notes will assist you in remembering the main factual information required to answer both AS and A2 questions.
- You should be able to identify and explain **different historical interpretations**. Most of the chapters in this book cover topics which have encouraged considerable

historical debate. It is important to know why historians have differed. They might have based their judgements on different evidence, written at different times or have a different philosophy or view on history.

- You will be asked to study and assess **sources in historical context**. To do this you have to have a good factual knowledge of the topic.
- In the A2 examination you will be expected to engage in **synoptic assessment**. This will require you to draw together different aspects of history to make a historical judgement. You might have to identify different political, social, economic and cultural reasons why a historical event occurred. You will also be expected to assess the role of the individual. Edexcel Unit 6 modules such as Chartism and the Decline of the Liberal Party require synoptic assessment.

How to prepare for the examinations

Effective planning of your revision will enable you to get the best out of the examination. Use a diary or calendar to plan the amount of time you intend to use for revision. It is much better to engage in revision over a period of time rather than all at the last minute. **Steady, methodical revision is always the best strategy.**

Examinations take place either in the morning or in the afternoon. Try to revise at a similar time. It is unwise to revise in the evening or late at night. You might eventually alter your body clock and, as a result, when you take an examination you might be mentally tired.

If you face a morning examination, give yourself plenty of time to get up and organise yourself. To prevent last minute hitches, pack all you will need for the examination the night before. Use these revision notes as a last minute memory prod to ensure that you have remembered the topics.

In the examination room

- Always take time to **read the examination paper carefully** to make sure that you answer the question on the paper.
- What are the **command instructions**? You may be required to explain 'why' or 'how' in an AS paper. In an A2 paper you might be asked to explain 'how far…?' or 'to what extent…?' You might also have to assess the validity of a statement.
- Are you being asked to cover a **particular period**? If the question states 1815–30, you will need to confine your answer to these years.
- Does the question contain any words or phrases which require **definition**? Make sure, for example, that you can define such terms as 'revolutionary', 'liberal' and 'conservative'.
- If the question is on a social or economic topic, try to include **statistical data** to support your case.
- Take a short time to **plan your answer**. This might be little more than writing down, in list form, the points you wish to cover. This will stop you forgetting important points.
- **Pace yourself.** Allocate your time so you spend an appropriate amount of time on each question. If, for example, you are sitting a 1-hour examination and one question is worth 30 marks and the other is worth 60, spend one third of the time (20 minutes) on the first question and approximately 40 minutes on the second question.

UNIT 1

The Tories in the age of Pitt and Liverpool, 1783–1830

KEY QUESTIONS

(1) How successful was Pitt the Younger in domestic affairs, 1783–89?

(2) How effectively did Pitt the Younger deal with the threat of revolution, 1790–1801?

(3) How did Lord Liverpool's government meet the challenges it faced, 1815–22?

(4) How liberal were the Tories, 1822–27?

(5) Why did the Tory Party disintegrate, 1827–30?

1 How successful was Pitt the Younger in domestic affairs, 1783–89?

1.1 BACKGROUND

By 1783, Britain had concluded the American War of Independence and was entering an era of political instability. Lord North had been prime minister since 1770 but in 1782 he was forced to create a coalition government with the leader of the opposition, Charles James Fox. The Fox–North coalition lasted from February to December 1783 and foundered largely due to George III's lack of support.

1.2 PITT THE YOUNGER

Pitt's long periods in office

William Pitt, aged 24, was appointed prime minister. Termed 'the Younger' to distinguish him from his father, William Pitt the Elder (the prime minister in the 1750s and 1760s, who later became Lord Chatham), Pitt the Younger was prime minister from 1783 to 1801 and from 1804 to 1806. The main reason for Pitt's long tenure in office was George III's support via the control of several hundred *placemen* in the House of Commons. Pitt also benefited from the growing fear of revolution after 1790, and from 1794 led a ministry which stressed the importance of law and order as a bolster against revolution.

General election, March 1784

In the March 1784 general election, 160 Fox supporters lost their seats and Pitt won a large majority. With the support of King George III, he dominated politics up to 1801.

1.3 FINANCIAL POLICIES

The move to stability

During the American War of Independence the national debt had doubled. Pitt was able to reduce public expenditure. Public loans were given out by tender, not by personal favouritism, and he introduced the effective *auditing* of public finances. Pitt's financial policies restored Britain's finances after the American War of Independence and he was able to increase trade and revenue through the lowering of some import taxes. By 1792, revenue was 47% higher than in 1783 and the government had a surplus of £1.7 million.

Financial legislation

Aided by peace with France and British industrialisation, Pitt introduced a range of measures which included:

- the Commutation Act, which lowered import duties on spirits and tea and increased trade by 1790 to the point where revenue on wines had increased by 29% and on spirits by 63%

- the Hovering Act, which extended the authority of customs officials to 12 miles from the coasts of Britain
- the Sinking Fund in 1786 where £1 million was set aside every year to accumulate interest in banks and pay off the national debt
- the 1786 Eden Treaty with France to lower duties on British manufactured goods and French wines. It lasted 6 years until the outbreak of war between Britain and France
- the abolition of sinecures and jobs for favours which had resulted in considerable over-manning in many government departments
- attempts to form a customs union with Ireland, an idea rejected by the Irish Parliament

1.4 OTHER POLICIES

The India Act, 1784
This Act created a Board of Control to monitor the performance of the East India Company.

Attempt at parliamentary reform, 1785
Pitt failed to reduce the number of *rotten and pocket boroughs*.

Size of the navy
Between 1784 and 1790, 33 new *ships of the line* were built and the navy increased from 15,000 to 18,000 men.

1.5 THE REGENCY CRISIS

George III suffered his first major period of mental incapacity in November 1788. Fox and the opposition tried to force through a bill to create a *regency* under the Prince of Wales who was an opponent of Pitt's. If successful, this would have led to the end of Pitt's ministry, but George III recovered sufficiently to keep his man in office.

2 How effectively did Pitt the Younger deal with the threat of revolution, 1790–1801?

2.1 BACKGROUND

When the French Revolution broke out in 1789, Britain initially welcomed the changes because the newly created constitutional monarchy reflected many features of Britain's political system. However, as the French Revolution became more extreme, Pitt's government feared a repeat of the French experience in Britain. The creation of a republic in 1792 and the beginning of the *Revolutionary Terror* created great concern in Britain. The execution of Louis XVI in January 1793 led to the outbreak of war between Britain and France.

From 1793 to 1801, Britain feared invasion by France. In 1797, a small French force landed at Fishguard in Wales but was easily captured. In 1798, a French military force succeeded in landing in Ireland to assist Irish rebels.

Consider how serious the threat of revolution in Britain was between 1790 and 1800, and how effectively Pitt's government dealt with the problem.

2.2 EVIDENCE OF REVOLUTIONARY ACTIVITY IN BRITAIN, 1790–1800

'The Rights of Man'

In 1791, the Englishman Thomas Paine published *The Rights of Man,* which advocated increased political liberty and supported the changes made in the French Revolution. The Priestley riots took place in Birmingham against supporters of reform and Nonconformists.

London Corresponding Society

In 1792, the London Corresponding Society was formed to encourage correspondence between supporters of political liberty. By 1795, other corresponding societies had been created and the London society had approximately 5,000 members.

Scotland

In 1793, a trial of radical reformers took place in Scotland, increasing fears of revolutionary activity in Britain.

Naval mutiny

Royal Navy sailors mutinied at Spithead and the Nore in 1797. Although the main reason for the mutiny was poor wages, it led to a fear of revolutionary activity in the armed forces.

Ireland

In 1798 a rebellion in Ireland was led by the United Irishmen, a secret society which had links with the French revolutionary government. Theobald Wolfe Tone, a leading United Irishman, was an officer in the French army. It took a considerable military effort to subdue the rebellion.

2.3 GOVERNMENT ACTION AGAINST REVOLUTION

Most discontent and radical protest was more to do with the economy than political radicalism. High food prices in 1795 marked the height of radical discontent and there were similar riots in 1801. However, the government's actions had the effect of forcing revolutionary activity underground. The following measures were passed:

- 1793 — the Aliens Act prevented French revolutionary agents entering Britain
- 1794 — the Habeas Corpus Amendment Act was suspended, allowing the government to arrest and imprison people without trial
- 1795 — the Treasonable Offences Act extended the crime of treason to include speaking and writing, and made it a crime to hold the king or the government in contempt
- 1795 — the Seditious Meetings Act required public meetings of more than 50 persons to be licensed by a magistrate
- 1798 — new taxes and government regulation of newspapers were introduced to prevent poorer people from reading about revolutionary ideas
- 1799 — ban on London Corresponding Society and United Irishmen
- 1799 and 1800 — *Combination* Acts made trade unions illegal
- 1801 — Habeas Corpus suspended a second time

2.4 THE WHIG FEAR OF REBELLION

Fear of revolution was sufficient to split the Whig Party in 1794. A group of Whigs under the Duke of Portland joined Pitt's government on the issue of defending law and order, and this greatly strengthened Pitt's position.

2.5 THE ACT OF UNION AND PITT'S RESIGNATION

The Act of Union, 1800, followed the Irish Rebellion. It created the United Kingdom by uniting Britain and Ireland and abolishing the separate Irish Parliament. As part of the political change, Pitt had promised Catholic emancipation, but George III's veto led to Pitt's resignation.

2.6 PITT'S FINAL TERM OF OFFICE

Pitt returned again as prime minister from 1804 to 1806 when his main contribution was to join a *coalition* against Napoleon and resume war with France. In 1805, Nelson's naval victory at Trafalgar prevented an invasion of Britain.

EXAMINER'S TIP

This topic is on the AS specifications of the OCR and Edexcel examination boards. You may be asked about evidence to suggest that Britain faced a revolutionary threat between 1790 and 1801. If so, you will need to explain what types of threat the government faced and the level of support revolutionary movements received. You will need to give reasons to support your views. You might have to explain the type of policy the government introduced to meet the possible threat of revolution. Even though the threat might not have been great, you should be able to explain that the government faced a problem which it feared might lead to revolution. You could contrast the problem in England with that in Ireland.

How did Lord Liverpool's government meet the challenges it faced, 1815–22?

3

3.1 SOCIAL AND POLITICAL UNREST, 1815–22

The Industrial Revolution

The introduction of machinery and the relocation of industry to large towns caused social problems. *Skilled workers* such as handloom weavers faced unemployment or a drop in wages. In addition, trade unions were illegal after 1799 and this limited the ability of workers to voice their grievances.

The end of the Napoleonic Wars

The end of war led to a rise in unemployment when 200,000 demobilised soldiers and sailors came onto the labour market and demand fell after the cancellation of government contracts for military clothing and weapons.

The Corn Law, 1815

The Corn Law aimed to protect British grain producers from foreign competition by placing an import tax on foreign grain. The result was a rise in the cost of living.

The lack of political reform, 1790–1815

Britain's participation in the French Revolutionary and Napoleonic Wars (1793–1815) put an end to political reform for the duration of the wars. When the wars ended in 1815, demands for political reform re-emerged.

3.2 CHALLENGES TO THE TORY GOVERNMENT, 1815–22

In the period immediately after the Napoleonic Wars, the Tory government faced many challenges.

Demonstrations and calls for reform
- The Spa Field Riots, 1816.
- The March of the Blanketeers, 1817.
- The Peterloo Massacre, 1819.

Attempts to overthrow central and local government
- The Pentrich Uprising, June 1817.
- The Perthshire Insurrection, 1820.
- The Cato Street Conspiracy, 1820.

Industrial unrest
- Luddism, 1816.

Political problems
- Queen Caroline Affair, 1820–21.

3.3 THE POSSIBILITY OF REVOLUTION IN BRITAIN, 1815–22

Political unrest

Many people feared that Britain was on the brink of revolution, but most of the challenges to the government were either local or economic in origin. *Luddism*, for example, was a reaction against the introduction of machinery into the textile industry, whilst the March of the Blanketeers was an attempt by cotton weavers to present their industrial grievances to the prince regent. Other challenges were political demonstrations which got out of hand, e.g. the Spa Fields Riots of 1816 and the Peterloo Massacre of 1819.

However, there were outbreaks of violent unrest. The Pentrich Uprising of 1817 and the Perthshire Insurrection were potentially serious outbreaks which were halted early in their development. The most serious outbreak was the Cato Street Conspiracy of 1820 when an attempt was made to assassinate part of the *cabinet* as a prelude to insurrection.

3.4 THE QUEEN CAROLINE AFFAIR

The most serious threat to Lord Liverpool as prime minister was not revolutionary. His government was rocked by the Queen Caroline Affair of 1820–21, which was caused by the estrangement of the prince regent, the future George IV, from his wife Caroline. He opposed his wife's claim to be crowned queen at his coronation in 1821. Lord Liverpool's handling of the issue caused a rift between the prime minister and his future monarch at a time when the monarch still possessed the power to dismiss prime ministers. When George IV was crowned in 1821, rioting in favour of Queen Caroline and against George IV resulted in the resignation of Lord Sidmouth the home secretary, and George Canning the president of the Board of Trade.

3.5 THE TORY GOVERNMENT RESPONSE

The nature of government

Government in the early nineteenth century was mainly local. The central government in London relied heavily on information from local officials in order to make its decisions, and many local officials exaggerated problems in order to get the central government to intervene. To supplement this source of information the central government used spies, the most famous of whom was Oliver the Spy (W. J. Richards) who helped stop the Pentrich Uprising.

In addition, most of the army that had defeated Napoleon had been demobilised and the central government only had a small army to maintain law and order. In the regions, law and order were maintained by a part-time militia.

Suspension of Habeas Corpus

In March 1817, the government suspended the Habeas Corpus Act following the Spa Field Riots of 1816. This meant that anyone suspected of radical or anti-government activity could be arrested and imprisoned without trial. However, it was a temporary measure. Suspension ended in 1818 and only a small number of suspects were arrested under its terms. It was a difficult decision by a government with limited resources to maintain law and order.

Peterloo Massacre

On 16 August 1819, the Peterloo Massacre followed a demonstration for political reform of some 60,000 people in central Manchester. Lord Sidmouth, the home secretary, had allowed the gathering for fear of provoking a riot if he had forbidden it. However, local officials brought in the *militia* to disband the demonstration, resulting in 11 deaths and 400 wounded. It prompted the introduction of the Six Acts, which included:
- censorship of the press
- limitations on demonstrations
- restrictions on the right to carry firearms
- speeding up the judicial process

Criticised by *radicals* at the time, these Acts were a sensible measure to meet what was seen as a dangerous situation.

cabinet: the main government decision-making body.

Luddism: a movement that attempted to prevent the introduction of machinery. Most prevalent in 1810–11 and 1816. Centred in Nottinghamshire.

militia: part-time armed force usually raised to repel invasion or keep law and order.

radical: used to describe anyone who wanted to see fundamental change in politics and society at the time, including political revolutionaries such as Arthur Thistlewood of the Cato Street Conspiracy, and Henry (Orator) Hunt, who wanted to use mass demonstrations to pressure the government into reform. The lack of unity and differences in ideas between radicals helps explain why the Tory government was successful in defeating the challenges it faced after 1815.

skilled worker: someone who had served an apprenticeship in a trade such as weaving or carpentry.

This topic appears at AS on the OCR and AQA specifications. It is an A2 topic for Edexcel. At AS you will be expected to explain why Britain faced political and economic problems from 1815 to 1821. You should place these in order of importance in terms of their impact on Britain. You should note that some problems were a serious political threat to the government. Others were peaceful protests or local in nature. In answering questions on the government's reaction, you should point out that the government at this time had no police force and limited ways of maintaining law and order. It also had to rely heavily on local government and local information to make and implement decisions. At A2 you will be expected to provide a balanced, analytical account. This could involve answering the question 'To what extent was Britain on the verge of revolution between 1815 and 1821?'

4 How liberal were the Tories, 1821–27?

4.1 GOVERNMENT CHANGES, 1821–23

Between 1821 and 1823 Lord Liverpool's government made the following changes:

- George Canning replaced Viscount Castlereagh as foreign secretary
- Sir Robert Peel replaced Lord Sidmouth as home secretary
- Frederick Robinson replaced Nicholas Vansittart as chancellor of the exchequer
- William Huskisson became president of the Board of Trade

However, these changes had little to do with any major shifts in government policy. Canning followed many of Castlereagh's ideas on foreign policy. Sidmouth resigned over the Queen Caroline Affair. Robinson had worked with Vansittart at the Treasury. If there was change in government policy, it was due mainly to a return to peacetime conditions following a long period of warfare and the adjustment to peace in the period 1815–22.

4.2 GOVERNMENT REFORMS, 1821–27

Lord Liverpool ignored the two most important political issues of parliamentary reform and *Catholic emancipation* because he knew these would split the Tory Party. However, the period saw many significant legislative changes.

Social reform

At the Home Office, Sir Robert Peel made major changes to the criminal (penal) law.

The number of offences carrying the death penalty was reduced. He also improved conditions in prisons.

Financial and trade reform

Robinson and Huskisson promoted the move towards free trade. Import taxes were reduced. *Reciprocity* Acts were made with important trading partners such at the USA. Indirect taxes were reduced in the *budgets* between 1821 and 1827.

Foreign policy

Canning was seen as less friendly towards Europe's conservative Great Powers than Castlereagh. (See Unit 2 Section 5.)

Trade unions

Trade unions were legalised with the repeal of the Combination Acts, 1824. However, the right to strike was still restricted through the Amending Act of 1825.

4.3 THE EFFECTS OF TORY CHANGES

Social reform

Peel's reforms at the Home Office merely brought British criminal law up to date. Offences which carried the death penalty, such as stealing a loaf of bread or damaging Westminster Bridge, meant many juries were unwilling to convict because of the harshness of the penalty. Reforms of the prisons were made after pressure from reformers such as William Howard and Samuel Romily.

Financial and trade reform

The trade and finance reform was a continuation of reforms introduced by William Pitt the Younger in the period 1784–90 and discontinued because of war with France.

Trade unions

The legalisation of trade unions was mainly the responsibility of the House of Commons. It followed the recommendations of a House of Commons Select Committee investigation into trade unions.

GLOSSARY

budget: a proposal explaining how the government plans to raise money to finance government expenditure.

Catholic emancipation: the right of Roman Catholics to sit in Parliament as MPs. This would affect parliamentary representation in Ireland where 80% of the population was Roman Catholic. Opponents feared it would destroy Britain's 'Protestant' political system.

liberal: featuring social, political and economic change. Compare with 'conservative' and 'reactionary', which mean opposing change.

reciprocity: a mutual agreement where both sides agree to adopt a similar policy.

EXAMINER'S TIP

This topic appears at AS for the AQA and OCR examination boards. It is an A2 topic for Edexcel. At AS you will be expected to explain the types of change the Tories introduced in domestic affairs. You may be asked to explain how liberal the Tories were. If so, you will have to provide a definition of the term 'liberal'. This type of question could also appear at A2. If you are asked why the Tories introduced reforms, you will be expected to place the reasons in order of importance. At A2 you may be asked to compare and contrast the

Tory government in domestic policy before and after 1821–23. The type of question you might be asked is 'To what extent was there a change in Tory policy after the cabinet changes of 1821–23?'

5 Why did the Tory Party disintegrate, 1827–30?

5.1 THE DEATH OF LORD LIVERPOOL, 1827

As prime minister, Liverpool had been effective at holding the Tory Party together. He avoided the issues of Catholic emancipation and parliamentary reform. He was succeeded by George Canning, who favoured Catholic emancipation. Both Peel and the Duke of Wellington refused to serve in his government as a result. When Canning died in 1827 he was replaced by Lord Goderich (formally Frederick Robinson), who failed to form a government and resigned after a few months. He was replaced by the Duke of Wellington, who was regarded as a reactionary Tory. Canning's followers, among them Huskisson, refused to serve in Wellington's government.

5.2 THE COUNTY CLARE ELECTION, 1828

A Roman Catholic, Daniel O'Connell, was elected as MP. This created a major political crisis over Catholic emancipation. The Wellington government faced the possibility of civil war in Ireland if Catholic emancipation was not introduced. The government passed the Catholic Relief Act reluctantly in 1829, allowing Catholics to sit in Parliament. However, the qualifications to vote in Ireland were raised to prevent most Catholics from voting. 142 *ultra*-Tories voted against the Act.

5.3 THE RISE IN SUPPORT FOR PARLIAMENTARY REFORM

By 1830, demand for the reform of Parliament had increased considerably. It was supported by radicals outside Parliament. Inside Parliament, Whigs and Canningites supported reform. In November 1830 a *coalition* of Whigs, Canningites and supporters of parliamentary reform replaced Wellington's government.

EXAMINER'S TIP

This topic appears on the AS specifications of the three major examination boards: AQA, Edexcel and OCR. At Edexcel it is part of Unit 3 on parliamentary reform. You will be asked to explain why the Tory Party disintegrated and will be expected to place the reasons in order of importance and to point out links between reasons. Catholic emancipation is in Unit 3 of the AQA specification, and you will be expected to write a course essay on this topic under exam conditions, although you are allowed to take in your own notes to help you with the essay. Make sure they are detailed. The information here gives you the basic material on which to base your course essay. For Edexcel you will be expected to place the disintegration of the Tory Party within the broader context of the demand for parliamentary reform.

KEY QUESTIONS

(1) How successful were the Whigs in domestic politics, 1833–41?
(2) How was Peel able to win the 1841 general election?
(3) How important were the economic, financial, social and Irish reforms of Peel's second ministry, 1841–46?
(4) Why were the Corn Laws repealed in 1846?
(5) How successful was Britain's foreign policy, 1815–41?

1 How successful were the Whigs in domestic politics, 1833–41?

1.1 THE WHIG PARTY

The Whigs formed a political party dominated by rich landowners. They had supported parliamentary reform between 1830 and 1832 in order to prevent revolution but were not radical social reformers. Following the 1832 election, the Whigs had a large majority over the Tories. However, they had to fight general elections in 1835, 1837 and 1841. After the 1835 election, the Whigs had to rely on support from Daniel O'Connell's group of Irish MPs and radicals. In 1839, the Whig government resigned following a revolt in Jamaica, but the Conservative leader, Peel, refused to take office because of the *Bedchamber Crisis*. Although the Whigs were reluctant reformers who ensured that participation in politics was limited to relatively few property owners, they made important administrative changes during their term of office from 1833 to 1841.

1.2 ABOLITION OF SLAVERY, 1833

The abolition of slavery in the British empire was largely the result of a long-running campaign led by William Wilberforce and the anti-slavery movement which happened to be passed during the Whig period in office.

1.3 FACTORY ACT, 1833

Lord Althorp's Factory Act was the result of a *Royal Commission* into factory conditions. It banned children under 9 years old from working, and those children between 9 and 13 years had to receive a minimum of 2 hours' education a day. The lack of a system of birth registration until 1836 limited the effectiveness of the Act. In addition, only four inspectors were appointed for the whole country, with one inspector responsible for all of northern England.

1.4 EDUCATION

The Whigs made the first government grant to education in 1833 and created the Education Department of the Privy Council in 1839. A sum of £20,000 per year was awarded to the Anglican National Society and to the *Nonconformist* British and Foreign Society for elementary education of children aged 5–11 years. This was significant because it eventually led to the creation of state education.

1.5 POOR LAW AMENDMENT ACT, 1834

This Act, which was the outcome of a Royal Commission, transformed state provision for the unemployed, elderly and infirm by introducing a uniform and national system which lasted until 1929. (See Unit 3 Sections 2 and 3 for more detail.)

1.6 MUNICIPAL CORPORATIONS ACT, 1835

A local government version of the Great Reform Act of 1832, this Act introduced elected local government in towns. Voting was based on property ownership. It meant that new towns, such as Birmingham and Bradford, got town government for the first time.

1.7 EARLY CENSUS

The compulsory registration of births, marriages and deaths in 1836 provided government departments with accurate statistics for the first time and facilitated more effective enforcement of legislation based on age limits, such as the 1833 Factory Act.

1.8 REFORM OF THE ANGLICAN CHURCH

The Anglican Church was the established or state church of England, Wales and Ireland. It received financial support from the government. The 26 most senior Anglican bishops sat in the House of Lords. In 1833, the Irish Church Temporalities Act reduced the number of Anglican clergy in Ireland. In 1836, the Established Church Act created new *dioceses* in Manchester and Ripon. It also created the Ecclesiastical (Church) Commission to look into future changes. The 1838 Pluralities Act prevented clergy working in more than one *parish*.

1.9 POSTAL SERVICE

Introduction of the Penny Post in 1840 was mainly the work of Rowland Hill rather than the Whig government and meant that the cost of post was paid for by the sender and not the receiver of post.

EXAMINER'S TIP

This topic is on the AS specification for OCR. The period 1833–41 is on AQA's AS specification. The whole period is also on Edexcel's A2 specification. At AS you will be expected to explain why the Whigs or the Conservatives introduced reforms. You should be able to place these reasons in order of importance and try to find links between reasons. You will also be expected to discuss how successful the Whigs were in domestic affairs. Both the Whigs and Conservatives had varying degrees of success — make sure you mention this. At A2 you will be expected to provide a balanced, analytical account. This involves producing a case for and against a question such as 'To what extent were the Whigs genuine reformers between 1833 and 1841?'

2 How was Peel able to win the 1841 general election?

2.1 PEEL TAKES OVER FROM WELLINGTON

Sir Robert Peel took over as Tory leader from the Duke of Wellington following the Tory Party's heavy defeat in the 1832 general election. Within 9 years, Peel had transformed the party and won the 1841 general election.

2.2 THE TORY PARTY BECOMES THE CONSERVATIVE PARTY

Peel accepted the changes made by the Great Reform Act of 1832 as the final change to the electoral system. He decided to win over support from the industrial middle class as well as to get support from more traditional Tory voters such as landowners and Anglicans. These new ideas were reflected in the change in party name to 'Conservative' in 1834.

2.3 TAMWORTH *MANIFESTO*

In this statement to the electors for the January 1835 general election, Peel stated that the Conservative Party would in future support reform of 'proven abuses'. Peel's party would also defend the Anglican Church, maintain law and order, and support the House of Lords and the monarchy.

2.4 THE 100 DAYS IN 1834–35

Peel's first *minority government* gave him the opportunity to put his new ideas into practice. His decision to set up a Commission into the Anglican Church is an example of this. Peel helped reorganise the party nationally. Using the terms of the Reform Act of 1832, he set up registration societies to register new voters.

2.5 PEEL'S REFUSAL TO TAKE OFFICE IN 1839

When the Whigs resigned over the Jamaica revolt in 1839, Peel used the Bedchamber Crisis as his reason to refuse to take office. He realised the Whig Party was in a process of decline and was rewarded with victory in the 1841 election.

2.6 THE WHIG PARTY LOSES POPULARITY

The rise of working-class unrest with Chartism from 1838 and the government's links with O'Connell's Irish Catholic Party were reasons for a loss of popularity with the electorate.

3 How important were the economic, financial, social and Irish reforms of Peel's second ministry, 1841–46?

3.1 BACKGROUND

Between 1841 and 1846, Peel's government laid the foundations for free trade. It reformed the banking system and introduced important social reforms in the mines and factories. However, his government's Irish reforms upset the Party's Anglican supporters. In addition, his free trade policy threatened the Corn Laws, which were supported by landowners.

3.2 FINANCIAL AND ECONOMIC REFORM

The Whigs left a deficit in government expenditure of £2 million.

Peel's first budget

In the 1842 Budget, Peel increased revenue by reintroducing income tax. This had only existed as an emergency tax during the French Revolutionary and Napoleonic Wars. It was introduced at 7d (3p) in the pound on incomes over £159 per year. This applied to only a small section of the population. It was meant to be for a 3-year period but became a permanent feature of the tax system.

Free trade

In the 1842 and 1843 budgets, Peel moved Britain further along the road to free trade by lowering tariffs (import duties). In 1841, there were over 1,200 items on which tariffs were charged. Peel removed 600 items from this tax and greatly reduced tariffs on 500 others. These reforms boosted government revenue by increasing trade. The reduction of tariffs on raw materials made British manufactured goods cheaper. It also reduced the cost of living.

Bank Charter Act, 1844

In the Bank Charter Act, 1844, Peel reformed the banking system, to bring stability to Britain's currency following financial crises in 1819 and 1826. The Act ensured:
- no new banks could issue bank notes
- when banks merged they lost the right to issue bank notes to the Bank of England
- all bank notes issued were backed by gold to provide confidence, except for £14 million known as a *fiduciary* issue

Bank of England

As banks merged, the Bank of England was the only bank in England that ended up issuing bank notes. This brought stability to the banking system during an important stage in the industrial revolution and also reduced the amount of currency in circulation, which encouraged the development of cheques as a means of payment. There were three banks in Scotland with the right to issue currency.

The Companies Act, 1844

This Act aimed to bring stability to business. It encouraged the growth of limited liability, which encouraged risk-taking, and made companies produce annual accounts.

3.3 SOCIAL REFORM

Peel's second ministry faced serious social problems brought about by the economic and social changes of the Industrial Revolution. The Chartist movement (see Unit 5) pressured the government for political reform. The economic depression of 1842 resulted in industrial unrest in northern England. The ministry passed two important social reforms in the Mines Act and the Factory Act. The Factory Act was controversial because education for factory children was to be in Anglican-controlled schools and it did not go far enough for *pressure groups* such as the Ten Hours Movement.

The Mines Act, 1842

This Act was the result of a Royal Commission set up by Peel and its effects were that:
- all children under 10 were forbidden to work in mines
- women were banned from working underground in mines

The Factory Act, 1844

This Act was mainly the work of the home secretary Sir James Graham and its effects were to:
- reduce working hours for under-13 year olds
- recommend improved safety in factories, such as fencing off machinery
- create opportunities for educating factory children

3.4 IRISH REFORM

The extent of the problem

Peel faced a major problem in Ireland and his attempts at resolving it were the most controversial of Peel's reforms. Most of the population were landless farm labourers engaged in subsistence agriculture. In addition, the vast majority of the population (80%) was Roman Catholic. The Irish politician Daniel O'Connell led the Repeal Movement and campaigned for the recreation of a separate Irish Parliament. Peel attempted to use firm tactics against the Repeal Movement and offered concessions to Roman Catholics, but his Irish Colleges Bill had the effect of upsetting both Anglicans and Roman Catholics.

The Devon Commission

The Devon Commission of 1843 investigated Irish land ownership and recommended improvements in the conditions of Irish labourers which were included in an Act of 1845. However, the Great Irish Potato Famine of 1845–49 destroyed any benefits the Act might have had.

The Repeal Movement

In banning O'Connell's 'monster' Repeal Meeting at Clontarf near Dublin in 1843, Peel took a hard line with the Repeal Movement and succeeded in reducing its influence.

Appeasing the Catholics

The appointment of Lord Heytesbury as lord lieutenant of Ireland in 1844 illustrated Peel's conciliatory policy towards Roman Catholics.

The Irish Colleges Bill, 1844

In this Bill, Peel attempted to establish *non-sectarian* university colleges in Belfast, Dublin and Cork. Though opposed by extreme Protestants and the Roman Catholic Church, the institutions were established as Queen's Colleges in 1845.

The Maynooth Grant

An increase of the Maynooth Grant provided money towards the training of Irish Catholic priests. It was opposed by many Anglicans, including Gladstone who resigned from the government.

This topic appears at AS for OCR. It is an A2 topic for Edexcel and AQA. At AS you might have to explain why Ireland was a problem for Peel or to assess Peel's role as prime minister. This would involve explaining how successful he was at dealing with the problems he faced. You should try to place Peel's achievements in order of importance. Mention his achievements, then any failures so that your answer has a balanced structure. At A2 more evaluative answers are required. The balanced, analytical account would require you to answer 'How far' or 'To what extent' types of question. You should also consider the different historical interpretations of Peel as prime minister.

4 Why were the Corn Laws repealed in 1846?

4.1 PROTECTIONISTS VS PEELITES

In 1846, the Conservative Party split into two factions. The *Protectionists*, under Lord Bentinck, wanted to keep the Corn Laws whereas the Peelites supported free trade. Supported by the Whigs, Peel repealed the Corn Laws. The decision was the natural culmination of Peel's financial and trade policy. In his budgets from 1842 to 1845 he reduced or removed hundreds of tariffs (import duties) on goods. Eventually, Britain would be a free trade country and the Corn Laws would be repealed.

Anti-Corn Law League

Peel and his government faced constant pressure to repeal the Corn Laws from the Anti-Corn Law League. This pressure group was based in Manchester and supported by manufacturers who wanted to lower the cost of living to make sure Britain benefited from free trade. It was led by John Bright, Richard Cobden and George Wilson and they used a variety of tactics — lecture tours, pamphlets and producing publications such as *The Economist*. They also pressured Peel in Parliament. Their main aim was to win a large number of seats at the forthcoming 1847 election.

4.2 THE IRISH FAMINE

The impetus for the Corn Law repeal was the Irish potato famine which began in 1845. Peel wanted to introduce cheap foreign grain to help the starving Irish *peasants* and this forced him to support repeal in 1846.

4.3 THE IMPACT OF REPEAL

Repeal of the Corn Law split the Conservatives, and the Peelites eventually joined the Liberal Party. Peel was accused of betraying his party because he:
- made concessions to Roman Catholics
- repealed the Corn Laws, which removed protection for British grain producers from foreign competition

Forced to choose between supporting industrialists and businessmen on the one hand and farmers on the other, Peel chose the former.

peasant: an agricultural worker who doesn't own land but rents it from a landowner.

protectionist: supporter of agricultural protection, i.e. keeping import duties on foreign grain.

This topic appears at AS for OCR. It is an A2 topic for AQA and Edexcel. When answering questions on causation you should try to place the reasons in order of importance. And try to see links between reasons. For instance, Peel's economic policy before 1846 and the demands of the Anti-Corn Law League are linked. You should also consider dealing with reasons in terms of time scale. What was the immediate reason which forced Peel to repeal the Corn Laws? What were the longer-term reasons leading him towards repeal? Remember, if you can provide different historical interpretations as to why Peel took this decision, this will add to the quality of your answer.

5 How successful was Britain's foreign policy, 1815–41?

5.1 THE MAIN INDIVIDUALS

British foreign policy was dominated by four individuals:
- 1812–22: Viscount Castlereagh (foreign secretary)
- 1822–27: George Canning (foreign secretary and prime minister)
- 1828–30: Duke of Wellington (prime minister)
- 1830–34;1835–41: Lord Palmerston (foreign secretary)

5.2 CASTLEREAGH'S FOREIGN POLICY, 1812–22

The defeat of Napoleon I

Castlereagh helped create the Fourth Coalition of Powers against Napoleon, and in 1812, Britain, Russia, Prussia, Austria and Sweden united to defeat Napoleon following his retreat from Moscow. Britain's main contributions were sea power, financing and supplying the armies of the other nations. Napoleon was defeated in the Peninsular War in Spain.

The Congress of Vienna, 1814–15

Castlereagh played a major part at the Congress to work towards a *balance of power* in Europe whereby no one *Great Power* could dominate the continent. He supported the *cordon sanitaire* around France with the formation of a United Netherlands, Prussian control of Westphalia and an expansion of Piedmont-Sardinia in Italy. Castlereagh helped maintain the balance of power by suggesting periodic meetings after 1815. This was Article VI of the Second Treaty of Paris and it created the Quadruple Alliance of Britain, Austria, Prussia and Russia. The meetings became known as the Congress System (1815–25).

Castlereagh also acquired Malta, the Ionian Islands, Heligoland, Mauritius, Ceylon and the Cape of Good Hope for the British empire. These acquisitions aided British sea power by providing naval bases.

The Congress System, 1815–22

Castlereagh worked closely with the other Great Powers at the Congress of Aix-la-Chapelle in 1818. However, in 1820 he took a different view from the others at the Congress of Troppau and refused to sign the Troppau Protocol, which gave the Great Powers the right to intervene against revolution anywhere in Europe. His alternative was the State Note of May 1820, which declared that Britain supported intervention in the internal affairs of other nations only when the balance of power was threatened. He supported Austrian intervention in Naples in 1821, but was against intervention in Spain and Greece.

Relations with the United States

Castlereagh was involved in the War of 1812 which led to his signing the following agreements:

- the Treaty of Ghent, 1814, where his signature ended the war and meant Britain recognised the independence of the USA
- a border agreement with the USA in 1818 which recognised the latitude 49° North as the Canadian–US border from the Lake of the Woods to Oregon
- the Rush–Bagot Agreement, 1819, which reduced naval and military facilities on the Great Lakes

Castlereagh opposed the Atlantic slave trade and placed a squadron of the Royal Navy off the West Africa coast to stop it. He claimed the right to search any ship on the high seas for slaves. This angered other nations.

5.3 CANNING'S FOREIGN POLICY, 1822–27

Canning's foreign policy was regarded as different from Castlereagh's, for they were supposed to have held different views towards the Congress System and relations with the USA. However, in many respects their foreign policies were similar.

The Congress System

Canning didn't like working closely with Metternich, the Austrian chancellor. He opposed intervention in Spain and Spain's former colonies in Latin America. After the Congress of Verona in 1822, Britain took no further part in the Congress System.

Beyond the Congress System

Canning continued to work with the other Great Powers when it suited Britain, as occurred over the Greek War of Independence (1821–32) when Canning worked closely with France and Russia to stop the conflict. In the Treaty of London, 1827, all three agreed to cooperate militarily and this led to the Battle of Navarino, 1827. Canning also intervened in Portugal in 1826 to support the liberal Queen Maria, who was an ally of Britain.

Trade

Canning supported the growth of British trade. He opposed intervention in Latin America because British merchants were trading successfully with the newly independent states. He was aided by US President Monroe's doctrine of 1823 which opposed European intervention in the Americas. Canning supported the suppression of the Atlantic slave trade.

5.4 WELLINGTON'S FOREIGN POLICY

In 1828 the Duke of Wellington became prime minister, and he was the major influence over foreign policy until 1830. Wellington failed to work closely with Russia over Greece. This led to Russian intervention in the Russo-Turkish War of 1828–29, which almost led to the collapse of the Ottoman empire in Europe.

5.5 PALMERSTON'S DEFENCE OF BRITISH INTERESTS OVERSEAS

Like Canning, Palmerston supported British trade, opposed slavery and defended the balance of power through the *Concert of Europe*. Between 1830 and 1841 he was involved in a number of foreign policy issues.

The Belgian Revolt, 1830–39

In the Belgian Revolt, Palmerston helped create an independent Belgium which had close links with Britain. He was able to persuade the other Great Powers to accept Belgian independence because Austria, Russia and Prussia were preoccupied with the Polish Revolt of 1830–31. The Treaty of London, 1839, created an independent Belgian kingdom and was an example of the Concert of Europe in operation.

The creation of a Greek kingdom, 1830–32

Another example of the Concert of Europe was the Treaty of London, 1832, which created an independent Greek kingdom following the Greek War of Independence.

The Middle East, 1831–33 and 1839–41

Palmerston faced two major Middle Eastern crises. In the first one Russia acquired the right to send warships through the Bosphorus and Dardanelles Straits into the Mediterranean. This threatened British sea power and precipitated a second crisis when Palmerston got the agreement reversed. In the Straits Convention of 1841 all the Great Powers agreed to keep the straits closed to warships.

Portugal and Spain

In Spain and Portugal, Palmerston supported the liberal claimants to the throne. In 1834 he signed the Quadruple Alliance with France, Spain and Portugal as a liberal alliance against conservative forces which could have disrupted British trade with the Iberian peninsula and with Latin America.

The Opium War, 1839–42

In the *Opium* War with China, Palmerston forced the Chinese government to allow more British trade, an act of aggression ratified in 1842 by the Treaty of Nanking. Britain also acquired the island of Hong Kong.

5.6 FOREIGN POLICY AIMS BETWEEN 1815 AND 1841

- Defence of British trade.
- Support for British sea power.
- Maintaining the European balance of power through the Concert of Europe.
- Opposition to the Atlantic slave trade.
- Making border agreements with the USA.

This topic appears at AS level for both the AQA and OCR examination boards. It appears as an A2 topic for Edexcel. The AQA specification requires coverage of 1815–30. The Edexcel specification requires coverage of 1815–27. At AS you will be expected to explain why Britain followed a particular foreign policy. You should place reasons in order of importance and try to find links between reasons. It is important that you know and can use key historical terms such as 'balance of power' and 'Concert of Europe'. A central feature of this topic is comparing and contrasting Castlereagh and Canning. You may decide that their style of foreign policy was very different but that they followed similar policies. You should also see links between the foreign policies of the different foreign secretaries, such as the way they handled the eastern question.

UNIT 3 Social and economic history, 1815–1914

KEY QUESTIONS

(1) What were the main issues, 1815–1914?

(2) Why was the Poor Law in need of reform, 1815–34?

(3) What impact did the Poor Law Amendment Act, 1834, have on the provision of poor relief?

(4) What impact did railways have on Britain?

(5) Why did the mid-Victorian boom take place, 1850–73?

(6) How did improvements in public health develop between the 1840s and 1870s?

(7) Why did industry and agriculture face depression from 1873?

(8) How did trade unions develop, 1850–1914?

1 What were the main issues, 1815–1914?

1.1 BACKGROUND

During 1815–1914 Britain experienced considerable social and economic change. Industrialisation meant the introduction of new production techniques and the relocation of industry. New jobs were created while old ones, such as handloom weaving, declined. Industrialisation led to the construction of factories and new industrial cities such as Leeds, Manchester, Birmingham and Bradford.

Industrialisation was aided by the development of transportation. In the early industrialisation period (1790–1840) the main form of industrial transportation was canals. From the 1830s railways replaced canals.

Britain's industrial development was not a smooth process. It faced periodic recessions or *slumps*. However, from the 1870s economic growth slowed considerably during a period known as the Great Depression.

As Britain industrialised, the relative importance of agriculture declined. As population increased, Britain became a net importer of food. From 1875 British agriculture faced a depression caused mainly by foreign competition.

2 Why was the Poor Law in need of reform, 1815–34?

2.1 BACKGROUND

The Poor Law provided assistance to the unemployed, infirm, old and young. The system had not been reformed nationally since its introduction in 1597 and 1601, and thus was very out of date.

2.2 ATTEMPTS AT IMPROVEMENT

Many attempts had been made to improve the system on a local and regional basis.

Knatchbull's Act, 1722

This encouraged parishes to build workhouses.

Gilbert's Act, 1782

This allowed parishes to separate the *able-bodied* from the infirm. Work was to be provided for the able-bodied poor.

Speenhamland System, 1795

This was introduced during a period of rising prices and was limited to southern England. It supplemented wages with money to help pay for higher food prices. This additional payment was calculated on the price of bread.

Sturges Bourne Act, 1819

This allowed parishes to appoint a Poor Law Committee with powers to determine the poor rate (tax) in their area.

The Roundsman System

This system, which existed intermittently throughout the eighteenth century, provided work for the poor during periodic slumps. It was most used in northern England.

The Royal Commission, 1833

By the 1830s, Britain had no national system of *poor relief*. It varied from area to area and was becoming increasingly costly. A Royal Commission on the Poor Law was formed under the dominating influence of *utilitarian* members, most notably Edwin Chadwick. The commissioners adopted a scientific method of inquiry, including the use of questionnaires.

EXAMINER'S TIP

This topic appears at AS or A2 for AQA and Edexcel and AS and A2 for OCR. In dealing with social and economic issues, you need to be able to use statistical data to support and sustain your arguments. The topic also appears in Unit 3 of the AQA specification for Alternative Q (Britain 1815–1914). Use the material in this section to construct detailed notes which you can use in a timed essay format.

3 | What impact did the Poor Law Amendment Act, 1834, have on the provision of poor relief?

3.1 BACKGROUND

The main aims of the investigators involved in the Royal Commission were to reduce the cost of poor relief and to cut agricultural able-bodied unemployment.

3.2 THE POOR LAW AMENDMENT ACT

The Act created a uniform system, and parishes were merged into Poor Law Unions which were large enough to finance and administer Poor Law workhouses. Each union elected a Board of Poor Guardians. The electors were the property-owning local *ratepayers*.

Poor Law Commission

A Poor Law Commission sat in London at Somerset House. Three main commissioners were appointed under Edwin Chadwick as secretary. Another layer of assistant commissioners worked under the guidance of the Poor Law Commission to supervise Poor Law implementation in the regions.

Workhouses

Outdoor relief was abolished. In order to make poor relief unattractive, the principle of 'less eligibility' meant that those who needed help had to enter a workhouse. Once in a workhouse, inmates had to work for their board and lodging. Married couples were separated in order to prevent them having children and imposing further burdens on the poor rates.

Anti-Poor Law Agitation

The new Poor Law established the idea that the main cause of able-bodied unemployment was personal defects in character, such as idleness. It did not recognise that unemployment was often the result of periodic economic slumps. The need to enter a workhouse to get relief was regarded by many as cruel and unrealistic. The Anti-Poor Law Agitation was created to fight the implementation of the new Poor Law and helped delay its implementation in parts of the north of England. The Anti-Poor Law Agitation later merged with the Chartist movement.

Outdoor relief continued to exist in the north during the depression of 1842. The administrative and construction requirements of the new Act also delayed implementation, and Norwich did not have a workhouse until 1859.

The new Poor Law was eventually introduced across the whole country by the end of the 1850s and greatly reduced the cost of poor relief.

National Insurance Acts, 1911

The 1834 Poor Law lasted until 1929, but the National Insurance Acts of 1911 took away many of its responsibilities in terms of unemployment and health matters.

GLOSSARY

outdoor relief: receiving Poor Law money or food outside a workhouse.
ratepayers: individuals who paid a local tax on property they owned.

EXAMINER'S TIP

This topic appears at AS for AQA and Edexcel and AS and A2 for OCR. For AQA it forms part of Unit 3, which is a timed course essay. Use the information in this section to make detailed notes which you could use in a timed essay. As you are dealing with the consequences of the Act, you should be able to place them in order of importance. Try to find links between consequences. You might also have to compare and contrast the Poor Law before and after the Poor Law Amendment Act.

4 *What impact did railways have on Britain?*

4.1 RAILWAY STATISTICS

In 1830, there were 98 miles of track. By 1850, there were 6,084 miles of track carrying 67 million passengers per year. By 1871, there were 13,388 miles of track carrying 322 million passengers per year.

The main era of railway building was the 1830s and 1840s. The main cities and towns of England, Wales and Scotland were joined by railways and in the 1860s and 1870s branch lines joined remoter areas into the national network. These included rural Wales and the Highlands of Scotland.

As railways developed, mergers took place between railway companies. By 1850, only 22 railway companies were in business compared to 200 in 1843. The rail network was dominated by large companies such as the Midland Railway and the London and North Western Railway. The Great Western Railway, built by Isambard Brunel, formed an autonomous unit until the 1890s. While most of Britain's railways adopted a railway gauge of 4 feet 8.5 inches, the Great Western had a gauge of just over 7 feet to allow the construction of wider trains.

4.2 GOVERNMENT AID TO THE GROWTH OF RAILWAYS

The early days

Until 1844, the railway network was built without any overall national plan or regulation. Instead, railways were built and operated by private enterprise with the result that many towns had several railway lines supplied by competing companies. London had a large number of railway terminuses: Paddington, Waterloo, Victoria, Cannon Street, Blackfriars, London Bridge, Fenchurch Street, Liverpool Street, Marylebone, St Pancras, King's Cross and Euston.

The Railway Act, 1844

Robert Peel's Conservative administration passed the Railway Act to create a Railways Board with the power to inspect railway safety. The Act also compelled railway companies to operate less profitable routes by running 'parliamentary' trains which stopped at all the stations on the line at a price of 1d (0.5p) per mile.

4.3 SOCIAL IMPACT OF THE RAILWAYS

The dramatic reduction in travel times meant the railway network transformed Britain in many ways. Among its effects were:
- abolition of different time zones within the country
- growth of national newspapers which could be printed in London by midnight and distributed throughout the country the following morning
- growth of the Royal Mail
- building of suburbs for city commuters
- building of new towns — Crewe and Swindon — based on the railway industry
- development of a national football league after 1888 — in 1874, the Factory Act created a free Saturday afternoon for most workers and this led to the growth of Saturday afternoon team sports such as football
- development of seaside resorts — the decrease in working hours also meant factory workers had the time for holiday breaks in places like Southport and Blackpool which were within an hour's journey from the *textile* mills of Lancashire

- growth of the professions and engineering industry
- changing of the landscape with embankments, bridges and stations; the construction of London terminuses such as Euston, King's Cross and Paddington also involved the destruction of large amounts of housing
- social unrest when *turnpike trusts* were forced to raise tolls as a result of railway competition — the Rebecca riots in South Wales are an example
- aiding the government in the suppression of Chartism by allowing the rapid movement of police to areas where Chartist disturbances were taking place

4.4 ECONOMIC IMPACT OF THE RAILWAYS

It is difficult to calculate the overall economic impact that the railway network had on the British economy, though recent estimates state that but for the railways it might have been 10% smaller. Whatever the precise impact, there are many examples of the way that the railways acted as a major driver of economic change:

- the construction effort which required thousands of workers — by 1847 approximately 300,000 navvies were building railways and, once their work was completed, more new jobs were created to run the system
- the spin-off economic effects of stimulating demand in the iron and coal industries
- encouraging innovation in engineering and industry by stimulating demand for new, more powerful railway engines, more sophisticated forms of signalling and better bridges
- the export of railway technology and expertise with the development of railways in Europe, India and the Americas
- encouraging investment, including a spate of 'railway manias', notably in the 1830s, when there was a rush to buy shares in railway companies
- bringing about the rapid decline of canals as Britain's main transportation system — to cut costs, canal companies reduced the wages of canal boatmen, which forced most of them to live on their boats
- broadening agricultural markets and stimulating the growth of towns, with food being transported quickly and efficiently into town centres
- stimulating the growth of *market gardening* around towns and cities

market gardening: growing crops for a local town, usually vegetables on a relatively small scale.

textiles: manufactured cloths such as cotton, wool and linen.

turnpike trusts: the road companies which built roads and made money by charging for their use.

This topic appears at AS for Edexcel, OCR (up to 1846) and AQA (up to 1841). You will be expected to explain the impact of the railways on Britain. As the notes illustrate, you can divide these into economic and social. Remember, it is important to understand the impact of railways on different aspects of the economy and society. As this is a social and economic topic, you should use statistical data, if possible, to support your views. Also try to include different historical interpretations on the role and impact of railways.

Why did the mid-Victorian boom take place, 1850–73?

5.1 BACKGROUND

Several factors combined to spur high levels of *economic growth*, though it must be noted that the period had its economic shocks. The most notable was in 1857 when a financial crisis brought a short, sharp downturn in economic activity.

5.2 FREE TRADE

Britain's gradual adoption of *free trade* between the 1840s and 1850s created the opportunity for the country to exploit world markets. Britain signed free trade treaties with the Ottoman empire in 1838 and France in 1860. As Britain was the most advanced industrial state, it could produce greater quantities of goods at lower cost than its international competitors.

5.3 RAILWAYS

The growing railway network aided the increased growth of the economy. It provided considerable employment plus opportunities for investment and increased demand for other goods such as iron and coal.

5.4 DEVELOPMENT OF INDUSTRY

The mechanisation of the textile industry by the 1850s greatly increased production and lowered costs. Textile production, particularly cotton textiles, was the major export earner in the British economy. The industry was adversely affected by the American Civil War in the early 1860s when supplies of cotton were disrupted. However, Britain quickly found alternative suppliers in Egypt and India.

5.5 POLITICAL STABILITY

Britain had a strong, politically stable government which provided the framework for economic growth.

5.6 LACK OF ECONOMIC RIVALS

Britain had industrialised ahead of the rest of Europe. This gave it the edge in manufacturing and cost of exports. The USA's emergence as a potential rival was disrupted by the American Civil War between 1861 and 1865.

economic growth: an increase in the wealth and production of an economy which is usually associated with a rise in gross national product.
free trade: an economic policy where no taxes are charged on imports or exports.

This topic appears at A2 on the AQA specification for Alternative Q (Britain 1815–1914). It will require you to place the reasons for the economic boom in order of importance. Try to find links between reasons. As this is an economic topic, you should use statistical data, if possible, to support your arguments. If you are aware of different historical interpretations, these should be included in an essay answer to support and sustain your argument. Remember, you need to understand historical terms such as boom, economic growth and gross national product. You may be asked to explain these in your answer.

6 ## How did improvements in public health develop between the 1840s and 1870s?

6.1 BACKGROUND

As Britain industrialised, it faced a number of social problems. Slum housing developed haphazardly in towns and cities, and the increase in town populations was not matched by developments in water supply or sewage disposal. In addition, there was no control of industrial pollution. Between 1848 and 1875, successive governments attempted to deal with public health.

The reformers faced many obstacles:
- central government had a laissez-faire attitude and generally favoured minimal government intervention
- local government disliked central government influence on its affairs
- factory and property owners saw legislation as a way of forcing them to make costly change

6.2 THE PUBLIC HEALTH ACT, 1848

There was a *cholera epidemic* in 1831–32 and 10 years later, in 1840, a Royal Commission reported on the living conditions of the urban poor. Another cholera outbreak in 1848–49 killed 90,000 people and was a factor in forcing the Whig/Liberal government of Lord John Russell to take action. The Public Health Act specified that once 10% of the local inhabitants had petitioned for a Local Health Board, local authorities could establish one. These local boards were supervised by a Central Board in London, which had the powers to:
- create local boards where there was local demand
- compel local authorities to set up a local board if the annual death rate in an area was at least 23 per 1,000

Apart from this, the Central Board had limited powers and while towns such as Leicester used the Act effectively to create a clean water supply, others ignored it. By 1864, over 400 towns had taken up powers granted under the Act. Cities like Liverpool and Manchester purchased land in Wales and the Lake District to build dams and ensure a supply of water.

6.3 THE PUBLIC HEALTH ACT, 1858

The Board of Health was closed down and its powers were transferred to a new medical department of the Privy Council and to local government offices. The effect was that local initiatives in public health were no longer subject to central control.

The most influential public health reformer after Edwin Chadwick was Sir John Simon. He was chief medical officer for the City of London from 1848 to 1855. In 1858 he was appointed medical officer to the Privy Council and he used his position to pressure the government towards compelling a uniform provision of public health. This helped lead to the passage of the Sanitation Act, 1866.

6.4 OTHER PUBLIC HEALTH ACTS

Sanitation Act, 1866

This gave the government power to insist that local authorities built sewers, provided a clean water supply and employed sanitary inspectors who were empowered to remove 'nuisances'. The Act was a turning point in government intervention in public health matters.

Local Government Act, 1871
An Act to establish Local Government Boards to supervise public health.

Public Health Act, 1872
This legislation made the appointment of medical officers compulsory for local authorities. Sanitary authorities were set up.

Rivers Pollution Act, 1875
This made provision to fine firms for polluting rivers. However, it had limited effect because the Act failed to provide an adequate definition of pollution.

The Sale of Food and Drugs Act, 1875
Under this Act it became an offence to adulterate food and drink. However, there were only a limited number of qualified chemists available to local authorities to test any complaints adequately.

The Artisans' Dwellings Act, 1875
This gave local authorities the authority to remove slum housing. Its most notable effect was in Birmingham under the leadership of Joseph Chamberlain. The Act was a *permissive* one and only 58 local authorities had used its powers by 1880.

The Public Health Act, 1875
This placed all previous public health legislation under one Act. It gave local sanitary authorities the power to enforce sanitary regulations, including drainage, sanitation and water supplies.

6.5 EFFECTS OF LEGISLATION
In 1870, the death rate was still 24 per 1,000. However, by 1901 the death rate had fallen to below 18 per 1,000. Nevertheless, epidemics still occurred. In 1892, Blackburn, Lancashire, was affected by a typhoid outbreak. In 1893, London had another cholera epidemic. Smallpox, diphtheria and scarlet fever all caused considerable infant mortality into the twentieth century. Only the mass immunisation campaigns of the 1950s and 1960s brought these diseases under control.

In 1914, the biggest killer of adults was TB (tuberculosis), a disease which thrived in poor housing conditions.

GLOSSARY

artisan: skilled worker.
cholera: a contagious disease caused by bacteria in polluted water.
epidemic: the rapid spread of a contagious disease.
permissive: lacking in compulsion.

EXAMINER'S TIP

This topic appears at AS for Edexcel. You should be able to explain the roles of Chadwick and Simon in trying to improve public health. In doing so, you should assess the degree of success they both achieved. In dealing with the success of public health changes, you should explain the importance of the different public health Acts passed. You should also be able to explain the obstacles faced by public reformers in achieving their aims.

7 Why did industry and agriculture face depression from 1873?

7.1 RISING UNEMPLOYMENT

The period between 1873 and 1896 was known as the Great Depression. Economic growth slowed from the average 3% growth rates during the mid-Victorian boom. On the eve of the Depression, in 1872, unemployment was 1%, but by 1879 it had risen to 11.9%. It remained at 10% during 1886 and there was rioting in Trafalgar Square in 1887. However, the levels of unemployment did not reach those after the 1929 slump.

7.2 CAUSES OF DEPRESSION

It is important to note that Britain wasn't the only country to face a slowdown in economic growth, for the downturn affected the rest of Europe and North America. Moreover, although industrial prices dropped and the economy slowed, a fall in the cost of living benefited those in employment. Britain suffered for two main reasons.

Increase in foreign competition

By the 1870s, both Germany and the USA had industrialised and the head start Britain had developed in the early part of the century had gone. In 1875, Britain had 35% of world steel production compared to 26% for the USA and 16.6% for Germany. By 1894, Britain's share had fallen to 24.6% while the USA's had risen to 33.7% and Germany's to 21.4%.

Introduction of overseas tariffs

By the 1890s, all Britain's major economic competitors had placed tariffs on imported goods. This limited Britain's ability to export. However, Britain kept free trade, which enabled foreign states to compete more favourably in British markets. Some countries such as Germany were guilty of 'dumping' — deliberately selling goods at low cost to undermine a rival's industry.

7.3 AGRICULTURE

Not all agriculture suffered. Market gardening around large urban areas grew rapidly, and falling industrial and agricultural prices meant the real wages of farm workers increased after 1875. The warnings of Corn Laws supporters didn't materialise and between 1854 and the mid-1870s Britain experienced a golden age of agriculture. However, from the mid-1870s to the First World War, agriculture went into *depression* for a variety of reasons.

Increased foreign competition

By the mid-1870s, large quantities of cheap American cereals entered Britain, causing a collapse of the domestic corn-producing industry. The cost of carrying a quarter tonne of wheat from Chicago, USA, to Liverpool fell from 55p to 21p between 1869 and 1892.

Bad harvests

The Richmond Commission on Agriculture reported in 1882 that low industrial yields were due to heavy rainfall between 1875 and 1879.

New technology

The development of canning and refrigeration ships meant that large quantities of Argentine and Australian meat could be imported into Britain, and by 1895, one third of meat was imported.

depression: an alternative name for a slump. A decline in economic growth associated with falling prices and rising unemployment.

This topic appears at A2 in the AQA Alternative Q (Britain 1815–1914). You will be expected to know and use correctly historical terms associated with the Great Depression such as economic protection, slump and dumping. In dealing with causation questions you should place and explain the reasons for the Great Depression in order of importance. You may be able to find links between different reasons. In a balanced, analytical answer you might have to compare the importance of one reason against the others. You shouldn't describe or attempt to write a story. Instead you should construct your answer in a for/against format in line with the wording of the question.

8 How did trade unions develop, 1850–1914?

8.1 BACKGROUND

Before 1850, trade unions faced considerable problems. They were illegal until 1824 and after that they were regarded as radical and potentially revolutionary. In the early 1830s the Tolpuddle Martyrs were transported to Australia for taking a secret oath to join a trade union. The Grand National Consolidated Trades Union (GNCTU) of the 1830s was an attempt to create a large, nationwide union. It collapsed because of effective opposition from employers.

8.2 NEW UNIONISM

New Model Unions

From 1850 a new type of union developed. They charged a high subscription fee to skilled members such as engineers, carpenters and boilermakers. They supported the Liberal Party and their main aim was to look after the welfare of members rather than to pressure for political change. The model for this type of trade union was the Amalgamated Society of Engineers, founded in 1850. In 1867, the *Hornby vs Close* court case concluded with a judge declaring that trade unions were not legal entities and had no legal protection over their funds.

Trade union legislation

The New Model Unions pressured Gladstone's Liberal government to make changes in the law, and in 1871 the Trade Union Act legalised trade unions. In the same year, the Criminal Law Amendment Act made it difficult for unions to strike. Then the Conspiracy and Protection of Property Act, 1875, gave unions the right to picket peacefully during strikes.

Other unions and strikes

New Model Unions were limited to a relatively small number of skilled workers, but in the late 1880s larger unions were formed amongst the unskilled. In 1888, a strike by workers at the Beckton Gasworks, East London, led to the creation of a Gasworkers' Union. In the same year, the matchgirls' strike, at the Bryant and May factory, led to the creation of a Matchgirls' Union, and in 1889 the London dockers' strike succeeded in gaining a pay rise. Although unskilled workers made considerable strides towards forming trade unions between 1888 and 1892, the 1890s saw an employers' backlash. Organised gangs were used to break strikes and disrupt trade unions. Employer lockouts occurred and court cases went against trade unions. Most famous was the Taff Vale decision in 1901, which declared that unions were responsible for a company's loss of revenue during a strike.

8.3 THE LABOUR REPRESENTATION COMMITTEE, 1900

The Labour Representation Committee (LRC) was formed to defend and represent trade union interests in Parliament. By 1906, it had 29 MPs and had changed its name to the Labour Party. It was responsible for the passage of the Trades Disputes Act, 1906, which reversed the earlier Taff Vale decision.

8.4 LABOUR UNREST, 1910–14

Textile workers, seamen, dockers, coal miners and railwaymen organised national strikes. The main cause was a rise in the cost of living, but opponents feared the militancy as a rise in *syndicalism*. In 1914, coal miners, railwaymen and transport workers formed the Triple Industrial Alliance which said that if one union went on strike, the others would follow suit to force a quick settlement.

GLOSSARY

syndicalism: a left-wing/socialist idea to bring down the government by industrial action (strikes).

EXAMINER'S TIP

This topic appears at AS for the OCR examination board (Trade Unions and Labour, 1867–1906). It also appears at A2 for AQA in Alternative Q (Britain 1815–1914). You will need to explain how different forms of trade union developed at different times. You should also explain the obstacles that existed to the development of trade unionism. Employers, the courts and the government should be considered here. As this is a social and economic topic, you should use statistical data, if possible, to support your arguments. These would be important in explaining the growth of trade union membership.

1 Why did many believe the electoral system was in need of change by 1830?

1.1 BACKGROUND

When deciding why the British electoral system was in need of change by 1830, the following points need to be taken into consideration:

- the distribution of seats in an electoral system which had changed little since the seventeenth century, in spite of major movements in population
- determining who had the right to vote in elections
- determining how elections were to be conducted

1.2 PARLIAMENTARY SEATS

There were two types of parliamentary seat: the counties (or constituencies) and the boroughs.

Counties

These were in England, Wales, Scotland and Ireland, the latter having been added after the Act of Union in 1800. Only one MP was elected from each county irrespective of its size, whether a large county like Yorkshire or a small one like Rutland. Qualifications to vote were based on ownership of land. Those who owned land worth £2 in rentable value per year (the 40 shilling freeholders) could vote, a practice which dated back to 1430.

Boroughs

These were usually associated with towns. Qualifications to vote varied from borough to borough and included:

- freemen who had received the freedom of a town or city
- potwallopers who cooked their midday meal over their own fire (e.g. Taunton, Somerset)
- scot and lot taxpayers who paid a tax to defend their town against Scottish invasion (e.g. Preston, Lancashire)
- burgage tenants who owned certain plots of land known as burgage plots
- those in corporation boroughs who had served on the town council

Due to the change in the distribution of population, some boroughs had very little or no population at all. Dunwich in Suffolk could only be seen at low tide; Old Sarum in Wiltshire was a mound with a few sheep; both returned two MPs to Parliament. These types of borough were called rotten boroughs and whoever owned the land there had the right to choose the MPs. These contrasted with boroughs such as Liverpool which had 5,000 electors in 1830.

Other borough constituencies were controlled by a local landowner. Voting was not secret and the election took several days. In the eighteenth century, pocket boroughs — where rich men could either bribe or intimidate the electors to vote for them — were a common feature.

The king had the right to create new borough seats and George III (1760–1821) exploited this privilege to increase his influence in the House of Commons. An example of this abuse was in Cornwall where, in 1831, a population of 300,000 returned 42 MPs. Meanwhile, the 1.3 million Manchester inhabitants returned just 14 MPs. Movements in population meant that several new industrial towns — Birmingham being the prime example — had no MPs.

1.3 SUPPORTERS OF CHANGE

Radicals

The radicals formed a broad group in support of major changes in Britain's social and political structure. They disliked the dominance of the landowning classes and wanted Parliament to be more representative of the British people. More extreme radicals wanted democracy and campaigned for one-man-one-vote. Others wanted the right to vote broadened to include factory owners, clerks and skilled craftsmen. Votes for women were not considered at this time.

The Whigs

The *Whig* Party had been out of power for much of the period from 1760 and needed a change in the method of elections if they were going to displace the Tories.

2 Why did the Whigs pass the Great Reform Act, 1832?

2.1 PARLIAMENTARY PROCEDURES

Before a proposal for change becomes law, a bill must go through various stages:

- the First Reading where an announcement is made that a proposal will be introduced
- the Second Reading where the principle of the bill is discussed and voted on
- the Committee Stage where the bill is discussed by a committee clause by clause and amendments are made
- the Report Stage when the bill is reported back to the whole House
- the Third Reading and the final stage of the bill's discussion in the House
- bills originating in the House of Commons are sent to the House of Lords to go through the same procedure and vice versa
- once it has gone through Parliament, the bill receives the Royal Assent and becomes law as an Act of Parliament

2.2 CANNING TAKES OVER FROM LIVERPOOL

The Tory Party disintegrated between 1827 and 1830. Lord Liverpool, who was prime minister from 1812 to 1827, successfully prevented discussion of parliamentary reform. Following his death, the Tory Party did not find a leader to unite the whole party. Canning in 1827 alienated the extreme or ultra-Tories, and Wellington from 1828 to 1830 alienated the Canningites. In November 1830, the Tories lost the election because many Canningites joined the Whigs.

Cautious reformers

Many people had the desire to rectify the worst abuses in the electoral system and to eliminate the worst rotten and pocket boroughs. They also believed that some adjustment to the system of election was required following the population movement caused by the industrial revolution.

Fear of revolution

From 1830 to 1832, popular support for change led the Whig government to believe that revolution would take place if some reform was not passed. These fears were based on the following:

- the July Revolution, 1830, which happened in France when Charles X's failure to grant political reform led to his being overthrown
- the Belgian Revolt, 1830, after which people in Britain feared that unrest might spread from the European mainland
- Thomas Attwood's General Political Union in Birmingham, a pressure group demanding electoral reform and supported by members of the middle and working classes
- the Captain Swing Riots of 1830–31, which took place in southeast England and were social in origin, being protests by agricultural labourers against the introduction of machinery and *tithes*
- Nottingham Castle was set alight by pro-reform demonstrators and the Bishop of Bristol was attacked in the street
- the May Days Crisis, 1832, when the Duke of Wellington formed an anti-reform Tory government
- Francis Place, a Political Union member, organised a bank panic in London which forced Wellington to resign

tithes: taxes paid to the Church of England.

This topic appears at AS for all three main examination boards: AQA, Edexcel and OCR. You will be expected to know and understand historical terms associated with the passage of the Reform Bill. It is important to know the different stages that a proposal for reform has to go through before it becomes law. In dealing with questions on causation, you will be expected to place and explain in order of importance the reasons why the Reform Bill was passed. It is also useful to find links between causes. You should avoid describing how the Reform Bill was passed.

3 What was the impact of the Great Reform Act?

3.1 BACKGROUND

The Act prevented the outbreak of revolution in Britain, but many of those who felt it was too moderate went on to create the Chartist movement.

3.2 THE CHANGES

- Many rotten boroughs were abolished. Fifty-six English boroughs with fewer than 2,000 voters lost both seats and another 31 small boroughs lost one seat.
- Several of these old seats were redistributed to new towns such as Birmingham, Manchester and Leeds.
- Twenty new constituencies were created.
- County representation was increased by 61 to 253.
- In the boroughs, a common qualification extended the vote to those who owned property worth £10 annual rent.
- In county seats, the right to vote of 40 shilling *freeholders* was retained. Owners of £10 *copyhold* land and £50 *leasehold* land were added.
- All voters had to register to vote.

3.3 EFFECTS OF THE CHANGES

The Great Reform Act was the first change to the electoral system since the seventeenth century and its passage through Parliament entailed a 2-year political crisis involving the resignation of three governments. King William IV threatened to create new peers if the House of Lords rejected the bill and — beyond the legislature — there was a considerable amount of demonstrating and violence.

Once the Act became law, it had the following effects:

- In a population of some 24 million, the electorate increased by 78% from approximately 366,000 voters to 652,000.
- In social terms the Act meant rich middle-class men could vote.
- Richard Cobden, a radical, said: 'It wasn't a good bill but when it was passed it was a great bill.' This suggests that the way the changes became law was more important than the changes themselves.

What didn't change?

- Elections were still not secret and took several days to complete. Bribery and intimidation were still commonplace.
- Many pocket and rotten boroughs remained.
- Politics was still dominated by a landowning class which made up the vast majority of the House of Lords. The Lords could still veto legislation and also dominated the House of Commons.
- MPs were not paid. Up to 1858, they had to own property to stand for election.

copyhold: a form of land ownership where the occupier holds land for a specific period of time. If he died within that period, he could hand on the land to another person, usually a relative.

freehold: a form of land ownership where the occupier of land has complete control over its ownership.

leasehold: a form of land ownership where the occupier owns land for a specific period of time. At the end of that time he has to renegotiate the lease or hand it back to the landowner.

This topic appears at AS for AQA, Edexcel and OCR. You should learn and use historical terms associated with the Reform Act and its impact. In dealing with the consequences of the Act, you should place and explain them in order of importance. Alternatively, you might wish to discuss and explain the consequences in order of time. You could start with the immediate consequences of the Act, then explain the long-term ones.

4   Why did the demand for parliamentary reform re-emerge, 1865–67?

4.1 EVENTS LEADING TO FURTHER REFORM

Garibaldi's visit to Britain, 1864

Italian unification increased the demand for more British parliamentary reform. When the Italian revolutionary leader Giuseppe Garibaldi visited Britain in 1864, his support for the idea of democracy caused great public excitement.

The impact of the American Civil War, 1861–65

The war divided opinion in Britain. However, support for the North was strong among most of the *working classes*, who saw the conflict as the victory of democracy over slavery and privilege.

The mid-Victorian economic boom from 1850

Britain went through a period of unprecedented prosperity. Increased prosperity had resulted in a 62% rise in the electorate since 1832, and the fear of revolution and social unrest had subsided. A large new class of skilled workers (artisans) was created and formed moderate trade unions called New Model Unions. They now demanded to be included in the electoral system.

The death of Palmerston, 1865

Palmerston had dominated British politics, and his opposition to any further parliamentary reform was an obstacle which could only be removed with his death.

Reform League

Popular support for more parliamentary reform led to the founding of the Reform League under Edmond Beales and George Howell. It combined *middle-class* and trade union support for reform and put pressure on Lord John Russell's government of 1865–66 to introduce a reform bill.

4.2 THE SECOND REFORM ACT, 1867

The period 1865–67 was associated with demonstrations for reform and economic crisis. A bank crisis and a poor harvest occurred in 1866. During 1867, there was rioting in Hyde Park and the Reform League kept up pressure on government. A Liberal proposal for parliamentary reform was defeated in 1866 because the Liberal Party split and Robert Lowe and many Whigs refused to give their support.

Eventually the Conservatives, under Derby and Disraeli, passed the Second Reform Act for the following reasons:

● to prevent a more radical measure being introduced

● to win support from the newly created voters (the Conservatives had not won a majority of seats since 1846)

● to respond to popular pressure, such as the Hyde Park riots

EXAMINER'S TIP

This topic appears as an AS topic for OCR and Edexcel and as an A2 topic for AQA Alternative Q (Britain 1815–1914). You will be expected to learn and use the historical terms associated with parliamentary reform. In dealing with causation, you should place and explain in order of importance the reasons why parliamentary reform became an issue and was passed in the mid-1860s. You might also try to find links between reasons. At A2 you might be asked to produce a balanced, analytical answer based on the discussion of the importance of one reason: for example, 'To what extent was the passage of the Second Reform Act due to pressure from outside Parliament?'

5 *What was the impact of the Second Reform Act, 1867?*

5.1 CHANGES IN THE RIGHT TO VOTE

● In boroughs, the vote was given to adult male home-owners who had lived in their house for more than 12 months.

- Lodgers who lived in houses worth more than £10 annual rent received the vote if they had lived there for more than 12 months.
- In the counties, owners of land valued at £5 per year leasehold were allowed to vote.
- Otherwise the situation was the same as after the 1832 Act.

5.2 CHANGES TO THE DISTRIBUTION OF SEATS
- Four seats were abolished due to corruption.
- Boroughs under 3,000 in population lost a total of 45 MPs.
- Towns such as Birmingham, Manchester, Leeds and Liverpool received more MPs.
- More seats were given to the counties.

5.3 THE SIZE OF THE ELECTORATE
The number of those eligible for the vote increased from 1,056,000 to 1,995,000, an increase of 89%. The main social change was the inclusion of skilled workers or artisans such as bricklayers, engineers, boilermakers and carpenters.

5.4 THE ORGANISATION OF POLITICAL PARTIES
The Act had a major impact on the political parties outside Parliament and spurred reorganisations in both the Conservative and Liberal parties.

The Conservatives
- A National Union of Conservative Associations started in 1867 to create a Conservative Association in each seat.
- Conservative Central Office began to coordinate a national party organisation in 1870.

The Liberals
- A National Liberal Federation was created in 1877. This united Liberal clubs in each seat and was modelled on Joseph Chamberlain's Birmingham Caucus.
- Chamberlain hoped the National Liberal Federation would have a major role in policy making within the party. This was blocked by Gladstone, the Liberal leader.

6 What impact did Gladstone's ministries have on parliamentary reform?

6.1 THE BALLOT ACT, 1872
This Act introduced the secret ballot at elections and at a stroke greatly reduced the possibility of bribery and intimidation.

6.2 THE CORRUPT AND ILLEGAL PRACTICES ACT, 1883

This Act laid down rigid rules for the conduct of parliamentary elections which included a limit on candidates' expenses and heavy penalties for bribery and intimidation.

6.3 THE REFORM ACT, 1884

In 1832 and 1867 three separate Acts had been passed for England, Scotland and Ireland and the 1884 Act was the first to apply to the whole United Kingdom. It brought changes to the size of the electorate and the right to vote.

Increased size of the electorate

The Act increased the size of the electorate from 3.1 million in 1883 to 5.7 million in 1885. In Ireland the electorate grew from 220,000 to 740,000 and this had an impact on the support for the *Home Rule* Party, which won 85 out of 105 Irish seats in the 1885 election. After the Act, 40% of the adult male population had the right to vote. Those adult males still without a vote included:

● domestic servants living with their masters
● unmarried men living with their parents
● soldiers and sailors
● many lodgers who didn't meet the residence qualification

The right to vote

The Act made the right to vote the same for borough and counties. Voting was still based on property qualifications and seven different ways of voting still remained. These included plural voting, where a person could have one vote for where he lived and another where he owned a business. Joseph Chamberlain had 26 votes. There were also university seats where graduates had a vote.

6.4 THE REDISTRIBUTION OF SEATS ACT, 1885

This was passed to gain support from the Conservatives for the 1884 Reform Act. Its effects were that:

● multi-member constituencies were abolished
● the idea that each seat should have a roughly equal number of electors was established and boundary commissioners were appointed to ensure this was followed

GLOSSARY

Home Rule: the creation of a separate Parliament for Ireland. Today the term used is devolution.

EXAMINER'S TIP

This topic appears at AS for OCR and A2 for Edexcel and AQA. At AS you might have to explain the nature and importance of the changes made to the electoral system. At A2 you might have to use your knowledge to answer source-based questions. If so, you will need to be able to place the sources in historical context. Also, you might be asked to produce a balanced, analytical answer which compares and contrasts the electoral system before and after these changes. Another likely question is to what extent these changes were a turning point in the development of democracy in Britain.

7 How did female participation in politics and elections develop, 1880–1914?

7.1 WOMEN'S ROLE IN LOCAL POLITICS BEFORE 1880

Before 1880 women's limited rights to take part in local politics had been defined within three pieces of legislation.

The Poor Law Amendment Act, 1834

This enabled women ratepayers to vote for Poor Law guardians.

The Municipal Franchise Act, 1869

This gave women ratepayers the same rights as male ratepayers in local elections. In 1872 this was changed to cover only unmarried women.

Forster's Elementary Education Act, 1870

This meant that women could vote for and be elected onto school boards.

7.2 DEVELOPMENTS IN FEMALE PARTICIPATION IN LOCAL POLITICS AFTER 1880

By the beginning of the twentieth century, over a million women had the right to vote in local elections and 1,147 women had been elected as Poor Law guardians. Some key post-1880 dates are as follows:

- 1888 — the County Councils Act gave female householders the right to vote in county council elections
- 1894 — the Parish Councils Act gave women the right to vote and to be elected to parish councils and rural district councils
- 1880s — the Conservative Party created the Primrose League for party activists and by 1900 over 500,000 of its members were women
- 1887 — the Women's Liberal Federation was created by Catherine Gladstone
- 1906 — the Labour Party established the Women's Labour League
- 1907 — the Qualification of Women (County and Borough Councils) Act allowed women to vote for and get elected to borough councils and county councils

7.3 ARGUMENTS USED TO DENY GIVING WOMEN THE VOTE BEFORE 1918

Family values

The world of work and politics was a male world and there was a belief that women's *suffrage* would destroy the family and undermine the Victorian family values that said a woman's place was in the home raising a family.

Stand by your man

A belief that married women would merely follow the political views of their husbands.

The apathy theory

A belief that women were indifferent to voting and that most did not want the vote.

The femininity argument

A belief that female suffrage would have an adverse effect on women, destroy their femininity and undermine the structure of society.

UNIT 4

suffrage: the right to vote.

This topic appears at AS for Edexcel and OCR and at AS and A2 for AQA Alternative Q (Britain 1815–1914) and Alternative R (Britain 1895–1951). At AS you might have to explain how women were involved in the political system before 1918 and why some people were opposed to allowing women to vote in parliamentary elections. You might also have to study sources. If so, you will have to use the information in these Revision Notes and your own notes to place these sources in historical context. If you have to produce extended writing, you will have to explain how far women were involved in the political process. This will involve explaining where women participated and where they did not.

8 What impact did the suffragettes have on the achievement of votes for women by 1918?

8.1 THE NUWSS

In 1897, Millicent Fawcett founded the National Union of Women's Suffrage Societies (NUWSS). They were known as suffragists and NUWSS members campaigned for the right of women to vote and stand in parliamentary elections. It aimed to win support through rational argument and moderate political pressure and had 50,000 members by 1914.

8.2 THE SUFFRAGETTES

In 1903, Emmeline Pankhurst and her daughters Christabel and Sylvia formed the Women's Social and Political Union (WSPU). Supporters of this organisation were known as suffragettes and they planned to win votes for women by more militant methods than the NUWSS.

The suffragette campaign reached its height between 1910 and 1913. Its tactics included setting fire to letter boxes, attacking politicians, slashing paintings in the National Gallery and going on hunger strike when imprisoned. The most controversial suffragette act was in the 1913 Epsom Derby when Emily Davison died by throwing herself under the King's horse.

The suffragette campaign began to decline following the passing of the Cat and Mouse Act, 1913. Suffragette hunger strikers were released from prison, then rearrested once they had eaten.

8.3 REASONS WHY THE SUFFRAGETTES FAILED TO WIN VOTES FOR WOMEN BEFORE 1918

Liberal reluctance

The Liberal governments of 1905–15 were reluctant to give votes to women because they realised that the process might have to be achieved in stages. Wealthy women might have to be given the vote first, which would have benefited the Conservatives.

Party splits

Both the Liberal and Conservative leadership were split on the issue. Lloyd George was in favour but Asquith, the prime minister 1908–15, was against. Neither political party was completely in favour of votes for women.

Other issues

Between 1909 and 1914 the Liberal government faced major issues over the House of Lords, Ireland, national strikes, and the *disestablishment* of the Anglican Church in Wales. Votes for women was a controversial issue which would have increased the government's commitments. This led to the defeat of the Conciliation Bill of 1912 on women's suffrage.

Politicians' reluctance to bow to direct action

The suffragette campaign had a negative effect on giving votes to women in that if the government had given women the vote, it would have been seen as giving in to militant action.

House of Lords opposition

The Lords was a male institution which was against votes for women. Before 1911 it had an absolute *veto* on all *legislation* and even after the passage of the Parliament Act, 1911, it could delay legislation for 2 years.

9 What impact did the Reform Acts of 1918 and 1928 have on the electoral system?

9.1 THE REPRESENTATION OF THE PEOPLE ACT, 1918

Even after the Act, between 5% and 7% of adult males still did not vote in the 1920s because they failed to register. The female vote greatly increased the size of the electorate and many women voted for the Labour Party, thus accelerating the decline of the Liberals in the early 1920s. Women entered the House of Commons for the first time in 1919, with Lady Astor (Conservative) representing Plymouth. In summary, the Act:

- gave the vote to women aged over 28 years
- abolished the property qualification to vote

- changed the residence qualification to vote to 6 months
- withdrew the vote from *conscientious objectors*
- redistributed seats, with extra seats being given to the counties around London
- increased the number of seats to 707, though this dropped in 1922 following the creation of the Irish Free State

9.2 THE EQUAL FRANCHISE ACT, 1928

This Act gave the vote to women over 21 years old and added 5.25 million voters to the electorate. Women now made up 52% of all those entitled to vote.

9.3 THE FIRST WOMAN MINISTER, 1929

Following the 1929 general election, Margaret Bondfield became minister of labour in the MacDonald Labour government.

GLOSSARY

conscientious objectors: men who refused to fight in the First World War, including pacifists who were morally or religiously against fighting and war.

EXAMINER'S TIP

This topic appears at AS for OCR and at A2 for Edexcel and AQA. You will be expected to learn and use historical terms associated with parliamentary and electoral reform. Material in these Revision Notes and other information you have acquired will allow you to place the sources in historical context. You might have to explain the significance of these reforms in bringing democracy to Britain. If so, you will be expected to compare these changes with the situation before 1918. You may also have to decide whether or not these Acts were a turning point in bringing democracy to Britain.

(1) What were the causes of Chartism?
(2) What roles did Lovett and O'Connor play in the Chartist movement?
(3) Why was Chartism popular?
(4) What methods did Chartists use to support their case?
(5) Why did Chartism fail?

1 *What were the causes of Chartism?*

1.1 POLITICAL ORIGINS

Chartism's immediate origins traced back to the eighteenth-century radicals who supported a major reform of Parliament as a way of changing who governed Britain. The Hampden Clubs formed during the Napoleonic Wars put forward views similar to Chartists, and between 1815 and 1821 radicals such as Henry Hunt demanded parliamentary reform. Many future Chartists campaigned for parliamentary reform between 1830 and 1832.

1.2 DISAPPOINTMENT WITH THE 1832 REFORM ACT

Although the Whigs regarded the 1832 Reform Act as the final change in the electoral system, the Act failed to give the vote to the working classes. (In some boroughs, such as Middlesex, working-class people actually lost the right to vote.) Chartists saw the Act as the beginning rather than the end of a process which would create democracy in Britain.

1.3 OPPOSITION TO THE NEW POOR LAW

The abolition of *outdoor relief* for the unemployed was unpopular, especially in northern England where there were periodic slumps in manufacturing. The Anti-Poor Law Agitation's failed attempt to stop the introduction of the Poor Law Amendment Act of 1834 convinced many people that, unless the composition of Parliament changed, this type of law could not be resisted or repealed.

1.4 THE IMPACT OF THE INDUSTRIAL REVOLUTION

Increased automation meant established jobs such as handloom weaving were threatened. In the late 1830s, there were 400,000 handloom weavers, mostly in the north, and they experienced a drop in wages. Chartism was popular amongst such workers.

1.5 ECONOMIC SLUMPS

In 1838–39, 1842 and 1847–48, Chartism gained in support to establish a direct correlation between the popularity of Chartism and economic *slumps*. After 1848, Britain experienced the mid-Victorian boom and Chartist support fell. This upholds the view that Chartism was a 'knife and fork' question, i.e. its aims were not so much political as social and economic.

1.6 THE GROWTH OF A RADICAL PRESS AND THE RAILWAYS

The rise in circulation of the *unstamped press* with newspapers such as the *Poor Man's Guardian* spread the ideas of Chartism, as did the growth of railways in the late 1830s.

outdoor relief: receiving Poor Law money or food outside a workhouse.

unstamped press: before 1861 all newspapers had to pay a tax. The unstamped press did not and were a form of illegal underground press.

This topic appears at AS in the AQA Alternative Q (Britain 1815–1914) and at A2 for Edexcel. Make sure you learn, understand and use the historical terms associated with the rise of Chartism. At AS you need to explain why Chartism developed and to place the reasons in order of importance. It would also be useful to find links between the reasons for the rise of Chartism. At A2 you will certainly be expected to find links between the various reasons for the rise of Chartism. This will allow you to engage in synoptic assessment. You will be expected to deal with the political, economic and social reasons for the rise of Chartism, and the role of individuals such as Lovett and O'Connor.

2 | What roles did Lovett and O'Connor play in the Chartist movement?

2.1 WILLIAM LOVETT

William Lovett was a moderate Chartist leader who was opposed to the use or the threat of violence. He helped create the London Workingmen's Association in 1836 and in 1838 he drew up the People's Charter along with Francis Place. Lovett reached the height of his influence in the movement between 1836 and the collapse of the National Convention and rejection of the First Petition in 1839.

2.2 FEARGUS O'CONNOR

Feargus O'Connor was the leading Chartist from 1840 to 1848 and the only Chartist parliamentary candidate to be elected to the House of Commons, for Nottingham in 1847. His main influence came through his control of the Chartist newspaper *The Northern Star* which had a circulation of 30,000 copies. He was a fine orator who raised expectations amongst Chartist supporters that simply could not be met.

O'Connor founded the Chartist Land Company in 1845 and attracted 70,000 share-holders who paid 1 shilling and 6 pence (7p) per share. When the company was wound up in 1851, it had organised only a few land holdings in Charterville, Oxfordshire, Great Dodworth, Worcestershire and O'Connorville, Hertfordshire.

This topic appears at A2 in both AQA Alternative Q (Britain 1815–1914) and the Edexcel specification. You will be expected to assess the role of these two individuals. Lovett's main role was in the creation of the Chartist movement. O'Connor's was in the growth, development and ultimate failure of the movement during the 1840s. At A2 you will need to compare the role of the individual with other reasons why Chartism rose and fell as a political movement.

Why was Chartism popular?

3.1 THE PEOPLE'S CHARTER

The People's Charter, after which Chartism took its name, united a wide variety of social and political groups. This can be explained, in part, by its demands which were:

- a vote for all males over 21 years
- a secret ballot at elections
- equal size for all parliamentary seats
- abolition of property qualification for MPs
- payment for MPs
- annual parliamentary elections

3.2 CHARTISM'S AIMS

The implementation of the above demands would have brought fundamental change to Britain by destroying rich landowners' control over Parliament. It would have allowed working-class men to enter the House of Commons. Those who supported Chartism looked forward to:

- the protection of the livelihoods of social groups such as handloom weavers
- the repeal of the Poor Law Amendment Act, 1834
- the establishment of democracy
- a redistribution of wealth from rich to poor

EXAMINER'S TIP

This topic appears at AS in AQA Alternative Q (Britain 1815–1914). It appears at A2 in the Edexcel specification. At AS you will be expected to explain why Chartism was popular. Avoid describing the Chartist movement. At A2 you will be expected to assess the reasons why Chartism was popular. You will need to draw together the different reasons why Chartism was popular with different groups.

What methods did Chartists use to support their case?

4.1 PETITIONS TO PARLIAMENT

Petitions to Parliament were an ancient constitutional right where, in theory, anybody could put pressure on Parliament to make changes. Three Chartist petitions were presented to Parliament in 1839, 1842 and 1848. The 1839 First Petition contained 1.2 million signatures, 1842's 3.3 million and, in 1848, just over 2 million signed the Third Petition. These petitions resulted in parliamentary debates on the People's Charter. Given the social composition of the House, it is not surprising that each debate resulted in a sound defeat for the Charter. What is more surprising is that some MPs voted in favour — 46 in 1839 and 49 in 1842.

4.2 POLITICAL ORGANISATION

The election of a Chartist National Convention in 1839 coincided with the First Petition. The Convention took its name from the French revolutionary body of 1792–95, emphasising the revolutionary nature of the organisation. It suggested a general strike (the 'sacred month') and also withdrawals of money from banks to induce a bank collapse, as had been organised successfully by Francis Place in 1832 to bring down Wellington's Tory government.

Other political organisations also rallied support for Chartism.

The New Charter Association

In 1840, the New Charter Association was founded in Manchester to provide central organisation for the whole movement. By 1842, it had 401 branches and a membership of 50,000. It had links with other pressure groups such as the Anti-Corn Law League.

The Complete Suffrage Union

In 1842, the Complete Suffrage Union was developed from the Birmingham Political Union of 1830–32. William Lovett was a leading member.

The Chartist Land Company

In 1845, the Chartist Land Company was founded to give every family who joined it a small-holding of 4 acres (1.8 hectares).

4.3 THE USE OR THREAT OF VIOLENCE

There were two serious outbreaks of violence and a bellicose newspaper associated with Feargus O'Connor.

The Newport Rising, 1839

In November 1839, after the failure of the First Petition to Parliament, John Frost and Zephaniah Williams organised an armed mob to attack the Westgate Hotel in Newport, South Wales. The rioters were dispersed by soldiers.

The Plug Riots, 1842

The *Plug Riots* were demonstrations, riots and strikes across northern England and the industrial Midlands culminating in the New Charter Association's vote to call a general strike across Britain.

The threat of violence

The Chartist leader Feargus O'Connor used his newspaper, *The Northern Star*, to highlight the dire consequences for Britain if the Charter was not accepted. He also organised mass demonstrations, the most famous of which took place on Kennington Common, south London, in 1848 as the prelude to the presentation of the Third Petition to Parliament. The government was alarmed enough to place the ageing Duke of Wellington in command of the capital's defence and special constables were raised to keep law and order.

GLOSSARY

petition: a list of signatures in support of an issue.
Plug Riots: the rioters removed the plugs from boilers, thereby preventing steam-worked machinery from operating.

EXAMINER'S TIP

This topic appears at AS in AQA Alternative Q (Britain 1815–1914). It appears at A2 in the Edexcel specification. At AS you will be required to explain why different Chartists supported different methods for trying to achieve the acceptance of the Charter. At A2 you will be expected to analyse these methods and determine why they failed to achieve their goal.

Why did Chartism fail?

5 (margin)

5.1 DISUNITY AMONGST ITS LEADERS

Chartism lacked strong leadership. In its early phase during 1838–39, William Lovett offered leadership. He was a moderate who was over-shadowed by the rise of Feargus O'Connor from 1840. Lovett left the movement in 1843 and O'Connor's leadership had limited impact. He lacked strong organisational skills and had to contain Chartist advocates of physical force such as Bronterre O'Brien and George Julian Harney.

5.2 DISUNITY AMONGST ITS MEMBERSHIP

Support for the Charter was the one thing Chartists had in common. Otherwise the movement was split regionally and its members among, say, handloom weavers, the unemployed, political radicals and opponents of the New Poor Law had little in common.

5.3 LACK OF MIDDLE-CLASS SUPPORT

Chartism lacked the financial and organisational strength which could have been offered by the middle classes. It stood in contrast to the Anti-Corn Law League, which was able to organise a national campaign that was properly funded and organised from a headquarters in Manchester.

5.4 THE RADICAL NATURE OF ITS AIMS

The Charter was far too revolutionary a proposal for Parliament to accept, for it would have led to the destruction of the political system then in existence.

5.5 THE MID-VICTORIAN BOOM, 1850–73

A sustained period of economic growth removed many of the economic grievances which had led to the development of Chartism in 1838–39, 1842 and 1848. As the demand for trades such as handloom weaving declined, so other employment opportunities arose.

5.6 THE STRENGTH OF THE BRITISH STATE

In Europe in 1848 many governments collapsed under the pressure of demonstrations and riots. In Britain the police and army remained loyal to the government. The Rural Police Act, 1839, ensured that a nationwide police force was in place to combat Chartism. In addition, the development of railways aided the swift movement of police and soldiers to areas of trouble.

In 1848, Russell's government made sure the Chartist demonstration would not get out of hand. In all, 7,000 soldiers, 4,000 police and 85,000 special constables were on duty when the Chartists gathered at Kennington Common.

The government was also swift to arrest and *transport* Chartist leaders to Australia. Over 4,000 Chartists were transported.

transportation: a punishment where those convicted were sent to Australia for a period of time. Once the sentence was complete, former prisoners would have to find their own way back to Britain. Most stayed in Australia.

This topic appears at A2 both in AQA Alternative Q (Britain 1815–1914) and in the Edexcel specification. It is important that you learn, understand and use historical terms associated with the failure of Chartism. You will also be expected to assess the reasons for the failure of Chartism in order of importance. In the synoptic assessment associated with Edexcel Unit 6 it is important to assess the political, social and economic reasons for the failure of Chartism together with the role of the individual.

The era of Gladstone and Disraeli — Liberals and Conservatives, 1846–94

KEY QUESTIONS

(1) Why was the Whig/Liberal Party dominant, 1846–65?

(2) What was Gladstonian liberalism?

(3) What domestic reforms did Gladstone's government pass, 1868–74?

(4) How successful was Gladstone's second ministry, 1880–85?

(5) Why was Ireland an important issue for Gladstone?

(6) Why were the Conservatives weak, 1846–65?

(7) How important was Disraeli to the development of the Conservative Party?

(8) What domestic reforms did Disraeli's second ministry pass, 1874–80?

(9) How successful was British foreign policy, 1846–65?

(10) What foreign and imperial problems did Gladstone face during his ministries of 1868–74 and 1880–85?

(11) How successful was Disraeli's foreign policy, 1874–80?

1 Why was the Whig/Liberal Party dominant, 1846–65?

1.1 BACKGROUND

The Whig–*Liberal* coalition held power during 1846–51, 1852–58 and 1859–65. The Conservatives only formed governments when there were Whig–Liberal splits in 1851–52 and 1858–59.

1.2 REASONS FOR WHIG DOMINANCE

Conservative weakness

Even though the Conservatives were the largest political group in the House of Commons between 1846 and 1865, they could not form a united front. Their split over the repeal of the Corn Laws led to the creation of the *Peelites* and the *protectionists*.

Coalitions

The coalition of Whigs, Liberals, Peelites and radicals was united in support of economic policy and moderate social reform and consistently outvoted the Conservatives.

Free trade

Gladstone was chancellor of the exchequer 1852–55 and 1859–65, and during these periods pursued an economic policy of free trade. He continued Peel's work in making Britain a free trade country and his 1853 budget removed virtually all import duties (tariffs). The mid-Victorian *boom*, 1850–73, also boosted Whig/Liberal popularity.

Palmerston's foreign policy

Palmerston was the dominant political figure between 1846 and his death in 1865. His seemingly aggressive foreign policy was supported by most of the electorate.

GLOSSARY

boom: a period of economic growth associated with rising prices and high levels of employment.

Liberal: political group which supported free trade, freedom of the press and the creation of a meritocracy.

Peelite: a follower of Sir Robert Peel within the Conservative Party, who supported the repeal of the Corn Laws.

protectionist: a Conservative who supported the retention of the Corn Laws.

This topic appears at AS in the OCR specification and A2 in AQA Alternative Q (Britain 1815–1914). It is important to learn, understand and use historical terms associated with the Whig/Liberal Party in this period. At AS you might be asked to explain the reasons why the Whig/Liberal Party was in power for most of the period 1846–65. At A2 you might be asked questions which require balanced, analytical answers comparing the importance of one reason for Whig/Liberal dominance with other reasons: for example, 'To what extent was the dominance of the Whig/Liberal Party due to the mid-Victorian boom?'

2 What was Gladstonian liberalism?

2.1 GLADSTONE'S POLICIES

Gladstone was the Liberal Party leader from 1866 to 1894 and adhered to the following political ideas.

Domestic policies
- Low taxation.
- Keeping the role of government and state intervention to a minimum.
- Reducing government expenditure, also known as 'retrenchment'.
- Increasing individual freedom and opposing privilege.
- Free trade in economic policy.

Foreign policies
- Using the Concert of Europe to support the European balance of power.
- Avoiding war and using *arbitration* to solve international disputes.
- Self-government for the white colonies of the empire.

2.2 GLADSTONE'S SUPPORTERS

The Gladstonian Liberal Party comprised a wide variety of different social and political groups. It was popular in large towns in the industrialised north and Midlands, and received considerable electoral support from Scotland and Wales. It also received a lot of support in Ireland before the rise of the Home Rule Party in the 1870s. Its supporters included the Peelites, Whigs, Nonconformists and Faddists.

Peelites
Former followers of Sir Robert Peel, of whom Gladstone was one.

Whigs
Rich landowners who led the Whig Party before the creation of the Liberal Party in 1859.

Nonconformists
Protestants who were not members of the Church of England. They wanted religious and civil equality with Anglicans.

Faddists

Liberal pressure groups that wanted change in a specific area, such as:

- the United Kingdom Alliance and Band of Hope Union, which wanted to limit the consumption of alcohol
- New Model Unions, which wanted to legalise trade unionism
- education reformers such as the National Education League, which wanted free, compulsory state elementary education
- land reformers

arbitration: a way of settling international disputes by submitting them to a third party to decide (arbitrate) on the issue.

This topic appears at AS in the OCR and Edexcel specifications for Unit 2. It is an A2 topic in the AQA specification. You should learn, understand and use historical terms associated with Gladstonian liberalism, such as 'meritocracy', 'faddism' and 'arbitration'. At AS you might be asked to explain why certain political and social groups supported Gladstone's Liberal Party. If you have to use and comprehend sources, you will need to use the information in these Revision Notes and other material you have acquired to place the sources in historical context. At A2 you may have to assess Gladstonian liberalism and be able to place and explain the reasons for its development in order of importance. You should note that the Liberal Party at this time comprised several competing social and political groups.

3 *What domestic reforms did Gladstone's government pass, 1868–74?*

3.1 BACKGROUND

Gladstone's first ministry attempted to remove privilege and create a *meritocracy*. His reforms covered a wide area of domestic policy and by 1874 had upset large sections of the electorate. This was an important reason for the Liberal defeat in the 1874 election.

3.2 IRISH REFORMS

The Disestablishment of the Church of Ireland Act, 1869

This Act took away the privileged position of the Anglican Church. It lost government funding and some of its land was sold. This removed a grievance of Roman Catholics who comprised 80 % of the Irish population.

The First Irish Land Act, 1870

This legislation gave Irish labourers compensation if they made improvements to land and were then evicted. It failed to cover eviction for non-payment of rent and had little overall effect.

Release of Fenian prisoners, 1870–71

An attempt to offer concessions to those who had organised the revolt against British rule between 1865 and 1867.

Irish Universities Bill, 1873

A failed attempt to create a non-sectarian university in Ireland where the government was defeated and Gladstone resigned temporarily.

3.3 OTHER REFORMS

The Forster Elementary Education Act, 1870

This Act created a national system of elementary education which was a mix of state-run (board) schools and church schools. Some Liberals opposed the idea of church-run schools and the Act's Cowper–Temple clause permitted parents to take their children out of religious lessons. Education was still neither free nor compulsory.

The Licensing Act, 1872

This licensing reform limited the opening hours of public houses. It was opposed by the brewing and distilling industries and supported by the Temperance Movement.

Trade union reforms

- The Trade Union Act, 1871, legalised trade unions.
- The Criminal Law Amendment Act, 1871, made it difficult for unions to strike.

Electoral reform

- The Ballot Act, 1872, introduced the secret ballot in elections.

Cardwell's army reforms

- Regiments were raised on a county-by-county basis to increase recruitment.
- The Martini-Henry infantry rifle was introduced.
- The size of the army was increased from 200,000 to 497,000.
- Commissions to be officers could no longer be bought.
- The War Office was reorganised into three departments under the commander-in-chief, the surveyor general, and the financial secretary. The commander-in-chief was placed under the direction of the war minister.
- British troops were withdrawn from the self-governing colonies.

Civil service reform

Competitive examinations were introduced for the home civil service.

The Supreme Court of Judicature Act, 1872

This entailed legal reform to reorganise English and Welsh high courts into Queen's Bench, Chancery and Probate, Divorce and Admiralty divisions.

3.4 ASSESSMENT OF THE REFORMS

These reforms removed privilege, modernised government and increased personal freedom. Several reforms were unpopular with parts of the electorate, notably:
- the Irish reforms upset Anglicans and landowners
- the Irish reforms also upset Irish nationalists, who believed they were too moderate, and this helped the rise of the Irish Home Rule party, which won 59 seats in the 1874 election
- the licensing reform upset both the brewers and the 'drinking masses'
- the abolition of the purchase of commissions in the army upset the aristocracy
- the Criminal Law Amendment Act upset the trade unions
- the Forster Elementary Education Act upset National Education League supporters

meritocracy: a society based on the idea that the most able and qualified people should receive the best jobs. A meritocracy is opposite to privilege, where the rich receive the best jobs irrespective of their ability.

This topic appears at AS in the Edexcel specification and at AS and A2 in the OCR specification. It appears at A2 in AQA Alternative Q (Britain 1815–1914). You should learn, understand and use historical terms associated with Gladstone's first ministry. At AS you should explain why reforms were passed and you may also be asked how successful these reforms were. If you have to use sources, use the information in this section and other information you have acquired to place sources in historical context. At A2 you will be expected to assess the success of the reforms. This might involve writing a balanced, analytical answer where you compare Gladstone's successes with his failures. You might be expected to explain how far his reforms of 1868–74 led to the Liberal election defeat of 1874. You might also be expected to mention different historical views on Gladstone's policies and reforms.

4 How successful was Gladstone's second ministry, 1880–85?

4.1 THE PROBLEMS GLADSTONE FACED

Gladstone's Cabinet was split between conservative Whigs and the *radicals*. They clashed over Ireland, the empire and social reform. Joseph Chamberlain, a leading radical, wanted to overhaul local government, and in 1885 he produced his own unofficial election manifesto, *The Radical Programme*. Gladstone's major problem was conflict over Ireland. During 1880–82 he faced an Irish Land War and in the House of Commons his government faced obstructionist tactics from the Irish Home Rule Party led by Charles Stewart Parnell.

4.2 THE REFORMS

Agriculture reform

In dealing with an agricultural depression, the Liberals:
- abolished the malt tax in 1880, which eased the tax burden on farmers
- introduced the Ground Game Act, 1880, which allowed *tenant farmers* to hunt hares and rabbits
- passed the Agricultural Holdings Act, 1883, to give tenant farmers more security of tenure

Education reform

The Mundella Act, 1880, made elementary education compulsory.

Women

The Women's Property Act, 1882, gave married women legal protection over their property.

Parliamentary reform

Gladstone's government passed three Acts, which are described more fully in Unit 4, Section 6. They were:

- the Corrupt and Illegal Practices Act, 1883
- the Reform Act, 1884
- the Redistribution of Seats Act, 1885

Irish reforms

- Coercion Acts gave the government the right to imprison without trial in an attempt to end the Land War of 1879–82.
- The Land Act, 1881, gave Irish tenant farmers the 3 Fs: free sale; fixity of tenure; and fair rent.
- The Kilmainham Treaty and the Arrears Act, 1882, brought an end to the First Land War of 1879–82.

4.3 GLADSTONE'S DEPARTURE

By the June 1885 general election, the Liberal government was split and Gladstone found it difficult to keep control of his party. The Irish Home Rule Party gained 86 seats in 1885, giving it the balance of power between the Liberal and Conservative parties. This forced Gladstone to resign and allowed Salisbury to form his first Conservative government.

5 | *Why was Ireland an important issue for Gladstone?*

5.1 BACKGROUND

Ireland was an important issue for a number of reasons:

- The majority of Ireland (80%) was Roman Catholic and until 1869 the established Irish church was the Protestant Anglican Church.
- Ireland was a predominantly agricultural country where most of the population rented agricultural land from a small number of landowners. This created conflict which resulted in attacks during the Land War of 1879–82.
- From 1870, the Irish Home Rule Party demanded the revival of a separate Irish Parliament in Dublin to look after Irish affairs.

5.2 THE TWO MINISTRIES

Gladstone's first ministry

Gladstone initially attempted to solve Irish problems by:

- disestablishing the Anglican Church in Ireland in 1869
- the First Land Act, 1870
- releasing *Fenian* prisoners, 1870–71
- the Irish Universities Bill, 1873
- *coercion*

Gladstone's second ministry

During Gladstone's second ministry, attempts at solving Irish problems were:

- the Second Land Act, 1881
- the Kilmainham Treaty and Arrears Act, 1882
- coercion

5.3 GLADSTONE'S SUPPORT OF HOME RULE

By 1885, the Irish Home Rule Party represented 75% of Irish seats in Parliament. In early 1886 Gladstone announced that he had decided to support Irish Home Rule and the creation of an Irish Parliament. Between 1886 and 1893, Gladstone twice introduced a bill to give Home Rule to Ireland. In 1886, he was defeated in the House of Commons and forced to resign as prime minister. In 1893, he was defeated in the House of Lords but remained as Liberal leader until his retirement in 1894.

There are various historical interpretations for why Gladstone supported Home Rule:

- Having tried and failed to solve Irish problems during his first two ministries, he came to the conclusion that only Home Rule would solve Ireland's problems.
- His belief that the 86 seats won by the Irish Home Rule Party in the 1885 election represented Irish opinion.
- His support of self-government for white, Christian peoples.
- His need to find an issue to unite the Liberal Party. Irish Home Rule won him Liberal support, but the Whigs and Joseph Chamberlain were opposed and split away to form the Liberal Unionist Party.

GLOSSARY

coercion: the ability to arrest and imprison without trial.

Fenian: a member of the Irish Republican Brotherhood. Founded in the USA in 1858, the IRB aimed to create an independent Irish republic by violent means.

EXAMINER'S TIP

This topic appears at AS and A2 in the OCR specification. It is an AS topic in the Edexcel specification and an A2 topic in AQA Alternative Q (British History 1815–1914). It is important to learn, understand and use historical terms associated with Gladstone and Ireland, such as 'coercion, 'Fenian', 'Home Rule' and 'Unionist'. At AS you might be asked to explain why Ireland was an important issue to Gladstone. Alternatively, you might be asked how successful Gladstone was in dealing with Irish affairs. At A2 you will be expected to write balanced analytical answers. These might involve comparing one reason for Gladstone's interest in Irish affairs with other reasons. Also at A2 there is considerable debate amongst historians about why Gladstone converted to Home Rule in 1886. In your answers to this question you could use these alternative views.

6 Why were the Conservatives weak, 1846–65?

6.1 BACKGROUND

In 1846, the Conservatives had split into bitter opposition between Peelites and protectionists. The majority of the leadership of Peel's Conservative Party joined the Peelites and their support of free trade meant they had more in common with the Whigs and Liberals than their old Conservative allies among the protectionists.

6.2 RIVAL GROUPINGS

Protectionists/Conservatives

The protectionist wing of the Conservative Party lacked strong leadership. During 1846–47 it was led by Lord George Bentinck and from 1847 to 1868 by the Earl of Derby who had more interest in horse racing than politics. From 1847, the Conservative leader in the House of Commons was Benjamin Disraeli. He was the only Conservative leader of any quality, but as a Jew he lacked strong connections with the landowning class and therefore had limited support from within his own party. Between 1846 and 1852, the party still supported *agricultural protection*.

The Whig/Liberal Party

The Whig/Liberal Party had strong leadership in this period with Lord John Russell (prime minister 1846–51) and Lord Palmerston (prime minister 1855–58 and 1859–65) dominating politics.

Anti-Conservative groups

The Peelites, Whigs and Liberals united to keep the Conservatives out of power for much of the period. Only when the coalition collapsed did the Conservatives form governments in 1851–52 and 1858–59.

GLOSSARY

agricultural protection: support for the Corn Laws.

EXAMINER'S TIP

This topic appears at AS in the OCR specification, Unit 2. It appears at A2 in AQA Alternative Q (Britain 1815–1914). At AS you might be asked to explain why the Conservatives were mostly out of power between 1846 and 1865. Compare Conservative weakness with Whig/Liberal strengths, which are mentioned in Section 1 of this unit.
At A2 you will be expected to produce balanced, analytical answers which might involve producing a case for and against a proposition in a question: for example, 'How far was the Conservative failure to hold office more frequently between 1846 and 1865 due to the leadership of Lord Derby?'

How important was Disraeli to the development of the Conservative Party?

7.1 DISRAELI

Benjamin Disraeli rose in importance within the Conservative Party following the split in 1846 over the repeal of the Corn Laws. In 1847, he became Conservative leader in the House of Commons and served as chancellor of the exchequer in Derby's three ministries of 1851–52, 1858–59 and 1866–68. He became prime minister in 1868 following Derby's retirement but lost the 1868 election to Gladstone. He was prime minister again in 1874–80. In 1876, he was made Earl of Beaconsfield, which meant he moved from the House of Commons to the House of Lords.

Following Disraeli's death in 1881, Conservatives credited him with founding modern Conservatism and Lord Randolph Churchill claimed Disraeli had established 'Tory democracy'. The Primrose League was founded in 1883 as a mass party organisation in Disraeli's honour and by 1912 it had 2 million members.

7.2 ORGANISATION

The Conservative Party was transformed under a Disraeli leadership which saw the National Union of Conservative Associations created in 1867 and a Central Office national headquarters established in 1870. Both worked closely together as a nationwide organisation led by the national agent, J. E. Gorst, who also initiated Conservative workingmen's associations, clubs and registration societies.

7.3 BROAD POLICY

Whereas the Conservatives under Lord Derby had been a Little Englander party, Disraeli looked overseas to defend the British empire and British interests abroad. In famous speeches at Manchester and Crystal Palace in 1872, Disraeli put forward the idea of the Conservatives as a *one-nation* party. He talked of elevating the condition of the people and also defended the monarchy and House of Lords.

GLOSSARY

one-nation Conservatism: the idea that the Conservative Party was supported by and gave support to all social classes.

EXAMINER'S TIP

This topic appears at AS for Edexcel and AS and A2 in the OCR specification. It appears at A2 in AQA Alternative Q (British History 1815–1914). It is important to learn, understand and use historical terms associated with Disraeli, such as 'Central Office', 'National Union' and 'Tory democracy'. If you have to analyse sources, use information from this section and other information you have acquired to place sources in historical context. At A2 you may be asked to write a balanced, analytical answer such as: 'To what extent was Disraeli the founder of modern Conservatism?' In such a question you should define 'modern Conservatism' as part of your analysis.

8 What domestic reforms did Disraeli's second ministry pass, 1874–80?

8.1 BACKGROUND

The Conservative government passed a large number of social reforms. Indeed, the Lib-Lab MP Alexander MacDonald said: 'The Conservatives did more for the working classes in 6 years (1874–80) than the Liberals did in 50.' Was this verdict correct?

8.2 THE REFORMS

Factory reforms

- The Factory Act, 1874, reduced working hours to 10 hours in 1 day and a half day on Saturday. This had an impact on the growth of Saturday afternoon sport.
- The Factory and Workshops Act, 1878, was the result of a Royal Commission into factories led by the home secretary, Richard Cross. It brought factories and workshops under government inspection.

Trade union reforms

- The Conspiracy and Protection of Property Act, 1875, reversed the Criminal Law Amendment Act, 1871, by allowing peaceful *picketing* during strikes.
- The Employers and Workmen Act, 1875, changed the law to make breach of employment contract a civil offence for employers and workers. Prior to that, workers who broke their contracts committed a criminal offence carrying a prison sentence.

Education reform

- Lord Sandon's Act, 1876, increased pressure on working-class parents to send their children to school by creating *truancy* inspectors. The aim was to help Anglican schools which faced falling numbers of pupils.

Economic reform

- The Friendly Societies Act, 1875, was the result of a Royal Commission set up by Liberals. It attempted to introduce registration of *friendly societies* in order to improve their financial stability.
- The Merchant Shipping Act, 1875, resulted from another Royal Commission set up by the Liberals. It introduced (non-compulsory) load lines on ships.

Agricultural reforms

- The Agricultural Holdings Act, 1875, gave compensation to farmers for improvements, but was permissive and lacked compulsion.
- The Enclosures Act, 1876, helped protect remaining areas of common land.

Licensing reform

- The Intoxicating Liquors Act, 1874, limited opening hours of pubs even more stringently than the Licensing Act of 1872.

Religious reform

- The Public Worship Regulation Act, 1874, attempted to stop the spread of Roman Catholic style religious ceremonies in the Church of England. It was disliked by many of the Conservative Cabinet, such as Lord Salisbury.

Social reforms

- The Artisans' Dwellings Act, 1875, allowed slum clearance in towns but was permissive and only used by a limited number of town councils.

- The Public Health Act, 1875, produced virtually nothing new but brought together all previous public health legislation into one Act.
- The Rivers Pollution Act, 1875, attempted to limit pollution of rivers but failed to provide an adequate definition of pollution.
- The Sale of Food and Drugs Act, 1875, came from a select committee report of the House of Commons which recommended limits to the adulteration of food and drugs. The Act failed to appoint qualified analysts to investigate possible abuses.

8.3 CRITICISM OF THE REFORMS
- Many of the reforms continued work begun by the Liberals under Gladstone.
- Much of the legislation aided Conservative supporters, such as the Church of England.
- Many of the Acts were permissive in character and a lack of compulsion limited their impact.

9 How successful was British foreign policy, 1846–65?

9.1 BACKGROUND
Lord Palmerston dominated foreign policy as foreign secretary from 1846–51 and prime minister in 1855–58 and 1859–65. His approach was that Britain had no permanent friends or enemies and should work with any country that would further British interests according to the following principles:
- preserving the European balance of power
- aiding British trade and British merchants
- using foreign policy issues to increase his own popularity at home

9.2 MAIN EVENTS
The Don Pacifico Affair, 1850
Palmerston (not Disraeli) defended the interests of British merchants abroad. Following a riot in Athens, the property of a British subject, Don Pacifico, was destroyed. Don

Pacifico was a Portugese Jew who had been born in Gibraltar, making him a British citizen. In retaliation Palmerston used the Royal Navy to blockade the port of Athens, and Greek shipping was confiscated until the Greeks gave Don Pacifico compensation. Palmerston defended his actions by claiming that British citizens throughout the world would be defended by the British government.

The General Haynau Affair, 1850

When London brewery workers assaulted the Austrian military *attaché,* Palmerston exploited the incident to increase his own popularity. He claimed Haynau had acted in a cruel manner in suppressing the Italian revolt in Lombardy in 1848–49 and deserved to be assaulted.

Louis Napoleon's coup d'état, 1851

Palmerston gave recognition to Louis Napoleon in France without informing the Cabinet. He calculated that Louis Napoleon's dictatorship would bring political stability and that this would further the interests of British trade.

Crimean War, 1854–56

Palmerston believed Russia was attempting to alter the European balance of power and came out in favour of declaring war on Russia in March 1854 and later — at the Treaty of Paris, 1856 — banning the Russian fleet from the Black Sea.

The Second Chinese War, 1856–58

Palmerston opened up China to more British trade by using the *Arrow* incident to declare war on China. The *Arrow* was a pirate ship operating in the Caton River against Chinese shipping. It had once been registered in British-controlled Hong Kong. When it was captured by the Chinese authorities, Palmerston declared war on China. In the Treaty of Tientsin, 1858, more Chinese ports were opened to British trade.

The Third Chinese War, 1859–60

An Anglo-French military expedition led by Admiral Hope forced the Chinese to accept the Treaty of Tientsin. It led to occupation of Beijing and ended with the Treaty of Beijing which ratified the Treaty of Tientsin.

Italian unification, 1859–60

Palmerston supported unification of Italy in the hope that a united Italy would balance French power in the Mediterranean. In 1860, Britain issued the Russell Dispatch, which warned European Great Powers against intervening in Italy and, in particular, blocking Napoleon III's attempt to prevent Garibaldi invading mainland Italy from Sicily.

American Civil War, 1861–65

- The *Trent* incident revealed Palmerston's tough line against the Northern government for arresting two Confederate representatives on a British ship. The intervention of Albert, the prince consort, prevented Palmerston sending an inflammatory diplomatic note to US President Lincoln and the issue was settled amicably.
- During the *Alabama* incident the British broke the Neutrality Act by allowing British-built warships to join the Confederate navy. This led to a deterioration in British–US relations.

Kagoshima, 1863

Palmerston used the murder of a British merchant as an excuse to bombard the Japanese port of Kagoshima. At a cost of 1,400 Japanese lives, Britain forced Japan to open up to trade.

Schleswig–Holstein affair, 1863–64

This was a failed attempt to prevent Austria and Prussia declaring war on Denmark over ownership of the north German duchies of Schleswig–Holstein, but Bismarck, the Prussian leader, called Palmerston's *bluff,* knowing that Britain lacked the military power to intervene.

attaché: a representative of a country attached to an embassy.
bluff: a threat which cannot be backed up.

This topic appears at AS and A2 for OCR and at A2 in AQA Alternative Q (British History 1815–1914). You should learn, understand and use historical terms associated with foreign policy, such as 'balance of power'. At AS you might be asked to explain the aims of British foreign policy. At A2 you will be expected to assess the degree of success of foreign policy. In particular, you might be asked to explain the significance of the Crimean War in British foreign policy. Remember, at A2 it is important to include different historical interpretations.

10 *What foreign and imperial problems did Gladstone face during his ministries of 1868–74 and 1880–85?*

10.1 GLADSTONE'S AIMS

Gladstone had the following aims in foreign and imperial policy:
- maintaining the European balance of power through the Concert of Europe
- solving international disputes through arbitration
- giving white colonies self-government within the British empire, in the belief that Britain had a moral duty to provide efficient administration

10.2 GLADSTONE'S FIRST MINISTRY, 1868–74

The Franco-Prussian War, 1870–71

The war was decided within a few months of its outbreak in September 1870 at the battle of Sedan. Gladstone's only intervention was to get an agreement by both sides not to violate Belgian neutrality. The Prussian victory completely altered the European balance of power.

Russia and the Franco-Prussian War

At the height of the Franco-Prussian War, Russia announced that it would cancel (revoke) the part of the 1856 Treaty of Paris that prevented it from building up a fleet in the Black Sea. Gladstone organised an international conference in London, where Russia was invited to apply for a cancellation of the Black Sea clauses. This was agreed.

The *Alabama* Award, 1872

This was a dispute from Palmerston's period that Gladstone sought to solve through international arbitration. A neutral court in Switzerland decided that Britain had to pay the USA compensation for allowing the *Alabama* and other warships to join the Confederate Navy in the American Civil War.

Empire: Gambia, Canada and New Zealand

In 1870, Britain planned to withdraw from the west African colony of Gambia. Gladstone also withdrew British troops from the self-governing colonies of Canada and New Zealand. Disraeli accused Gladstone of trying to dismember the British empire.

Empire: South Africa

In 1872, Gladstone granted self-government to Cape Colony. This was part of his policy of offering internal self-government in the empire. A government and parliament were created which were dominated by the white South African population.

Empire: the Ashanti War, 1872–74

Gladstone was forced into sending a military expedition to west Africa to protect the British Colony of Gold Coast (Ghana) from attack by Ashanti chief Coffee Calcalli. This led to the acquisition of west African territory to protect the Gold Coast.

10.3 GLADSTONE'S SECOND MINISTRY, 1880–85

By the end of his second ministry Gladstone had greatly increased British influence in Africa. He had not planned to expand the empire and did so reluctantly, being forced into action by events rather than following any overall plan.

Afghanistan, 1880

When Gladstone became prime minister he withdrew troops from Afghanistan, having accused Disraeli of getting Britain involved in costly colonial wars during the Midlothian election campaign of 1879–80.

First Boer War, 1880–81

Gladstone's decision to continue British rule of the Transvaal sparked off a brief war with the *Boers*, which Britain lost. At the Treaties of Pretoria, 1882, and London, 1884, Britain was forced to recognise Transvaal independence. A British belief that it controlled the Transvaal's foreign policy helped start the Second Boer War in 1899.

London Conference, 1880

Using the Concert of Europe, Gladstone called an international conference to deal with border disputes in the Balkans and Montenegro. It was agreed to give Thessalay to Greece.

Egypt, 1882–85

Following an Egyptian nationalist uprising against foreigners, Gladstone's government decided to invade Egypt in 1882. The main reason for intervention was to protect the Suez Canal and British investments in Egypt. Britain was forced to act alone because of political instability in France and this caused a major rift between the two countries.

Sudan, 1883–85

Sudan had been under Egyptian rule and in 1883 a fundamentalist Islamic revolt broke out. Led by the *Mahdi*, it destroyed an Anglo-Egyptian army. The government sent General Gordon to help organise a withdrawal, but he decided to stay in Khartoum even though it was surrounded by the Mahdi's troops. A relief force arrived too late to save Gordon, and Gladstone was blamed for not acting earlier.

Bechuanaland, 1885

Gladstone, urged by Joseph Chamberlain, took over the Kalahari Desert area of South Africa and acquired the Bechuanaland Protectorate. It was mainly done in response to the German acquisition of South West Africa in 1884–85 and to prevent Germany and the Transvaal having a common border.

Berlin West Africa Conference, 1884–85

Britain — along with Germany, France, Spain and Portugal — agreed to divide up west Africa into spheres of influence.

India, 1883–85

Gladstone's Indian viceroy, Lord Ripon, attempted to improve relations with the Indian population by introducing the Ilbert Bill in 1883. This would have allowed some educated Indians to become judges, but the bill was withdrawn after opposition from many British in India. The Ilbert Bill upset British and Indians alike and led to the creation of the Indian National Congress in 1885 to fight for Indian rights.

Penjdeh incident, 1885

In 1885, the Russians captured the Afghan town of Penjdeh. This threatened Britain's position in northwest India. It briefly created a major international crisis between Britain and Russia. To defuse the situation, Gladstone submitted the dispute to international arbitration. Penjdeh was awarded to Russia.

EXAMINER'S TIP

This topic appears at AS and A2 (up to 1880) in the OCR specification. It appears at A2 in AQA Alternative Q (British History 1815–1914). You should learn, use and understand historical terms associated with Gladstone's foreign policy, such as 'balance of power', 'Concert of Europe' and 'arbitration'. At AS you might be asked to assess the success of Gladstone's policies. If you have to use sources, remember to place them in historical context in your answers. At A2 you might be asked to compare the foreign policies of Gladstone's first two ministries. You might also be asked to explain how far Gladstone was a reluctant imperialist. Remember at A2 to try to include different historical interpretations.

11 How successful was Disraeli's foreign policy, 1874–80?

11.1 BACKGROUND

During Disraeli's short first ministry, in 1868 Britain sent a military expedition to Abyssinia (Ethiopia) to rescue British merchants. In the Manchester and Crystal Palace speeches of 1872 Disraeli stated his desire to defend the empire and British interests abroad. He criticised Gladstone's policies of 1868–74 and hoped to follow a policy similar to Lord Palmerston. In colonial affairs Disraeli delegated responsibility to 'men on the spot' and British involvement in southern Africa and Afghanistan was not directly his work.

11.2 MAIN EVENTS

Acquisition of Fiji, 1874

Disraeli followed advice from Colonial Office officials and completed a development begun during Gladstone's first ministry.

Suez Canal, 1875

Facing personal bankruptcy, the ruler of Egypt (the Khedive) attempted to raise money by selling his shareholding in the Suez Canal Company. Using a £4 million loan from his friends the Rothschilds, Disraeli bought the shares and only then sought Cabinet approval. The Khedive purchase gave Britain a major shareholding in a transport artery which had become a major sea route since its opening in 1869.

The Royal Titles Act, 1876

India had been made an empire by the Government of India Act, 1858, following the Indian Mutiny. Disraeli made Queen Victoria Empress of India to increase her prestige and to emphasise British rule in India.

Southern Africa, 1877

The colonial secretary, Lord Carnarvon, wanted to strengthen British control of the Cape of Good Hope and created a *confederation* of south African states from the British colonies of Natal and Cape Colony, and the Dutch Republic of the Transvaal.

The Balkan Crisis, 1875–78

This was the most important issue facing Disraeli and almost brought Britain into war with Russia. In the early part of the crisis, 1875–76, Disraeli attempted to disrupt the Three Emperors' League (the *Dreikaiserbund*) between Germany, Austria-Hungary and Russia, an agreement he thought was detrimental to Britain's European interests.

From 1877, Britain adopted a strong anti-Russian stance following the outbreak of the Russo-Turkish War. The Russians defeated a Turkish army in the Balkans and reached the outskirts of Constantinople, the Turkish capital. Disraeli intervened by sending the Royal Navy to Constantinople and British Indian army troops to Malta. British action forced the Russians to make peace. However, the peace treaty of San Stefano virtually destroyed Turkish rule in Europe and created a large pro-Russian Balkan state in Bulgaria.

The Treaty of Berlin, 1878, was the outcome of an international conference involving the five Great Powers. By the treaty, Disraeli succeeded in reducing the size of Bulgaria, saved the Turkish empire in Europe and acquired Cyprus for Britain. Britain also guaranteed Turkish borders in Asia. Gladstone criticised the treaty because he believed Britain couldn't defend Turkey's Asian borders and because he supported the independence of the Christian Balkan peoples.

The Zulu War, 1878–79

Sir Bartle Frere, the British high commissioner in southern Africa, was mainly responsible for getting Britain involved in a war with the Zulus in Natal. British troops suffered a humiliating defeat at Isandhlwana before pushing on to conquer the Zulu kingdom.

The Afghan Wars, 1878 and 1879

Though Gladstone blamed Disraeli for costly and unsuccessful colonial wars in Afghanistan, the main responsibility lay with Lord Lytton, the British viceroy in India.

confederation: a political union made up of a number of states.
Dreikaiserbund: Three Emperors' League of Germany, Austria-Hungary and Russia. It was formed in 1873 to defend the monarchy. It was similar to the Holy Alliance of 1815–1855 where Prussia, Russia and Austria attempted to control European international relations.

This topic appears at AS and A2 in the OCR specification and at A2 in AQA Alternative Q (British History 1815–1914). At AS you might be asked to explain Disraeli's aims in foreign policy. At A2 you might be asked to produce a balanced analytical answer which assesses Disraeli's performance in foreign and imperial affairs, such as 'How far was Disraeli personally responsible for foreign and imperial policy during his second ministry?' At A2 try to include different historical interpretations in your answers.

UNIT 7 Ireland, 1798–1998

KEY QUESTIONS

(1) What problems were created by Ireland for British governments, 1798–1867?
(2) How successful was Gladstone in dealing with Irish problems, 1868–93?
(3) How successful were the Conservative governments 1886–1905 in dealing with Irish problems?
(4) What impact did the Ulster Crisis of 1912–14 have on British–Irish relations?
(5) How did the Easter Rising of 1916 lead to a major change in British–Irish relations?
(6) Why was Ireland partitioned in 1920–22?
(7) Why did the Northern Ireland Troubles begin in 1968?
(8) How did British governments try to bring peace to Northern Ireland, 1972–98?

1 What problems were created by Ireland for British governments, 1798–1867?

1.1 IRISH PROBLEMS IN 1798

Parliament within the British empire

In 1798, Ireland was part of the British empire. Since 1782, the Parliament in Dublin had passed laws which could not be overridden by Britain's Parliament in London.

Catholic majority

Unlike the rest of the British Isles, Ireland had a large Catholic majority. Following the Jacobite Wars of 1688–91, Irish Catholics faced discrimination under the Penal Laws and were forbidden to own land or join a profession. However, by 1798, the Penal Laws were not effectively enforced.

Agricultural economy

Unlike the rest of the British Isles, Ireland had not industrialised and was a predominantly agricultural country of landless farm labourers engaged in subsistence farming.

Ireland's strategic position

Ireland posed strategic problems for Britain's defence. Geographically it lay across the sea routes into Britain.

1.2 THE 1798 REBELLION

United Irishmen

The French Revolution inspired the formation of the United Irishmen, a group which wished to create a rebellion in Ireland in order to establish a French-style republican government. An important figure linking the United Irishmen with France was Theobald Wolfe Tone.

French support of Ireland

In 1798, Britain was at war with revolutionary France. French plans for an invasion of Ireland in 1797 were thwarted by bad weather. In 1798, the French again planned an invasion in support of an Irish Rebellion.

Demands for equality

Catholics wanted to gain equality, as did the Nonconformist Presbyterians in the northeast of Ireland. They both opposed the Anglican Church — the established or state church which received financial support from the government.

1.3 THE IMPACT OF THE 1798 REBELLION ON BRITISH–IRISH RELATIONS

Suppression

The Irish Rebellion was savagely suppressed and thousands of people were executed.

The Act of Union, 1800

The Act of Union created the United Kingdom of Great Britain and Ireland. Ireland lost its Parliament. In future Ireland was to be ruled from London.

Catholic emancipation until 1829

Plans to introduce Catholic emancipation as part of the Act of Union were vetoed by George III and subsequent Catholic demands to sit in the House of Commons were a major political issue in British politics until 1829.

1.4 CATHOLIC EMANCIPATION, 1829

The Catholic Association

An Irish Catholic lawyer, Daniel O'Connell, organised the Catholic Association in 1823. It was the first mass political organisation in British history and tens of thousands of Irishmen paid a small subscription to provide funds to fight for Catholic emancipation.

Canning succeeds Liverpool

As prime minister from 1812, Liverpool had managed to avoid the question of Catholic emancipation. When he died in 1827 his successor, Canning, took a different line and this split the Tory Party, which disintegrated into pro and anti-Catholic emancipation factions between 1827 and 1829.

County Clare election

In the County Clare election, 1828, O'Connell won against Vesey Fitzgerald, a pro-Catholic emancipation Protestant. It created a political crisis — if O'Connell had been denied a seat in the House of Commons, it could have sparked off civil war in Ireland.

Catholic Relief Act, 1829

Peel, an opponent of Catholic emancipation, agreed to the passage of the Catholic Relief Act, 1829, because he feared revolution in Ireland if it was not passed. The Act granted Catholic emancipation. Opponents believed the Act would destroy the unity of the United Kingdom and undermine the Church of England's role in uniting the country.

1.5 O'CONNELL'S EFFECT ON BRITISH POLITICS, 1829–47

The Irish Party

In 1829, O'Connell formed the Irish Party in the House of Commons and — following the 1835 general election — joined the Lichfield House Compact with the Whigs.

Municipal Corporations and Poor Law Amendment Acts

Between 1835 and 1841, O'Connell was able to get the Whigs to extend the Municipal Corporations and Poor Law Amendment Acts to Ireland.

The Repeal Association

During Peel's second ministry, 1841–46, O'Connell created the Repeal Association. The aim was to restore Ireland's Parliament in Dublin by repealing the Act of Union. He tried to intimidate the government by holding 'monster' meetings calling for repeal. In 1843, Peel's government banned the 'monster' meeting at Clontarf near Dublin. This resulted in the rapid decline of the Repeal Movement.

Young Ireland Movement

O'Connell's political influence declined after the outbreak of Irish famine in 1845 and the rise of the Young Ireland Movement. This was a group of young Irish nationalists who wanted to create an independent Ireland.

1.6 MAIN ISSUES, 1845–68

Irish potato famine, 1845–49

In a population of around 8.5 million, the famine resulted in the deaths of approximately 1 million people and the emigration of another 1 million, primarily to Britain and America. Irish emigration changed the population structure of cities such as Liverpool and Glasgow, and the Catholic population in Britain increased rapidly. The Irish population continued to decline due to mass emigration until the late twentieth century.

Land ownership

Demands that landless labourers should have greater security over the land they farmed was a major issue in the 1850s and 1860s and led to the foundation of the Irish Tenants Rights League and the Independent Irish Party in Parliament.

Religion

Some 80% of Ireland's population were Catholic, 10% were Nonconformist Protestants and the remaining 10% were Anglicans. Yet the Anglican Church was the established or state church and all Irish people had to pay tithes towards its upkeep.

The Fenians

The Irish Republican Brotherhood (Fenians) was formed by Irish emigrants in the USA in 1858. The IRB planned to create an independent Irish Republic by violent means and — following the end of the American Civil War — the Fenians planned an uprising in Ireland, an invasion of Canada from the USA and bomb outrages in England. By 1868, the Fenian movement had been defeated by the British government and the IRB remained a secret underground society.

2 *How successful was Gladstone in dealing with Irish problems, 1868–93?*

2.1 BACKGROUND

During the 1868 general election Gladstone stated that he wanted 'Justice for Ireland'.

2.2 GLADSTONE'S FIRST MINISTRY, 1868–74

Disestablishment of the Irish Church Act, 1869

The Disestablishment of the Irish Church Act was Gladstone's attempt to bring religious peace to Ireland by ending the Anglican Church's special status.

The Land Act, 1870

Gladstone attempted to increase tenant security by extending Ulster land law to the rest of Ireland and giving compensation to evicted tenants if they had made land improvements. The Act did not apply to cases of non-payment of rent and collapsed under the effects of the Agricultural Depression from 1877 and the accompanying *Land War*.

Coercion

In 1870–71, Gladstone resorted to force and introduced arrest and imprisonment without trial in the effort to restore peace to the Irish countryside.

Prisoner amnesties

Gladstone organised the release of Fenian prisoners and their return to Ireland to help remove a grievance.

The Irish Universities Bill, 1873

This was an attempt to improve university-level education in Ireland. It tried to prevent controversy by excluding modern history, theology and philosophy from the curriculum. The Bill was opposed by Liberals, Catholics and Conservatives and its parliamentary defeat by three votes led to Gladstone's temporary resignation as prime minister.

2.3 GLADSTONE'S SECOND MINISTRY, 1880–85

The Land War

A Land War in Ireland involved gangs of labourers murdering landowners and their agents and maiming livestock.

Home Rule Party

Created in 1870, the Home Rule Party wanted the repeal of the Act of Union and a return of Ireland's Parliament. Charles Stewart Parnell led a disciplined organisation which adopted obstructionist tactics in the House of Commons. These caused such a disruption of government business that there was a change in the rules governing parliamentary debate.

United Irish opposition

Under Parnell's leadership, the Home Rule Party, the Land League in charge of the Land War and Irish Americans formed a single united organisation from 1879.

Gladstone's response

- The Land Act, 1881, giving Irish tenants the 3 F's of free sale, fair rent and fixity of tenure. It was rendered inoperable by the Land War.
- A policy of coercion including the arrest and imprisonment without trial of Parnell and other Irish leaders in 1882.
- The Kilmainham Treaty of 1882, an attempt to end Land War by releasing Parnell from prison in return for the abolition of all rent arrears by Irish tenants.

2.4 GLADSTONE'S CONVERSION TO IRISH HOME RULE

When Parnell's Home Rule Party won 86 parliamentary seats (75% of the Irish total) in the 1885 general election, Gladstone came to the view that Parnell represented Irish opinion. He believed this would lead to the natural culmination of his plans to bring peace to Ireland and he attempted to unite the Liberal Party behind his leadership by dumping the Whigs and Joseph Chamberlain.

2.5 Gladstone's failure to pass Home Rule

Gladstone's proposal to unite the Liberal Party on a Home Rule platform in 1886 split the party when 96 Liberals defected to form the Liberal Unionist Party. His opponents included:

- Irish Protestants who were involved in anti-Home Rule riots in northeast Ireland during 1886
- those who feared that Home Rule would split the United Kingdom and weaken the British empire
- those who feared that Home Rule would lead to Catholic domination of the Dublin Parliament
- those who feared that Home Rule would damage Ireland economically by dividing it from the more prosperous Britain
- the House of Lords, which had an absolute veto and rejected Gladstone's Second Home Rule Bill in 1893

3 How successful were the Conservative governments 1886–1905 in dealing with Irish problems?

3.1 Conservative opposition to Home Rule

The Conservatives used 'constructive Unionism' in an attempt to 'kill Home Rule with kindness'. This involved several elements.

Land Purchase Acts

In 1885, 1886, 1891 and 1903, the Conservatives passed Land Purchase Acts, which provided cheap loans to allow the landless Irish labourers to buy out their landlords. The aim was to create a class of small landholders who would no longer be attracted to Home Rule. The Acts achieved a quiet revolution in the Irish countryside.

The Crimes Act, 1887

This legislation followed precedent by providing a coercive stick to go with legislative carrots. The Act gave the police extensive powers of arrest and imprisonment. It brought about the Land League's Plan of Campaign, or Second Land War, after 1887.

The Congested Districts Act, 1890

This Act gave financial support in so-called *congested districts* for industrial and economic development in the west of Ireland.

Devolution Crisis, 1905

The Irish civil servant Sir Anthony MacDonnell announced that the government might accept a limited form of devolution and Irish self-government. The suggestion caused an uproar and led to the creation of the Ulster Unionist Council.

3.2 THE GROWTH OF IRISH NATIONALISM

In 1891, the Irish Home Rule Party had split over a scandal surrounding Parnell's divorce case and comprised pro- and anti-Parnell factions. In 1900, the Irish Home Rule Party reunited under the leadership of John Redmond and by the 1906 general election it was coherent enough to win 83 seats. During the years leading up to that election victory, several new political names emerged.

Gaelic Athletic Association

Formed in 1888 to preserve Irish field sports such as hurling and Gaelic football, this association also provided a political focus by encouraging support for Irish nationalism.

Gaelic League

In 1893, the Gaelic League was formed to prevent the decline of the Irish language.

Sinn Fein

In 1905, Arthur Griffith formed Sinn Fein (it means 'ourselves' in Irish). Its aim was to create a new political settlement based on the example of Austria-Hungary, which envisaged two independent countries joined together by a common monarch.

4 *What impact did the Ulster Crisis of 1912–14 have on British–Irish relations?*

4.1 THIRD HOME RULE ACT, 1912

The plan to create an Irish Parliament seemed to have reached fruition with the passage of the Third Home Rule Act in 1912. However, the House of Lords used its veto to delay the Act by 2 years and the Ulster Crisis of 1912–14 and tensions associated with the outbreak of the First World War prevented the implementation of a peaceful political solution.

Opponents of Home Rule

In an attempt to destroy Home Rule, politicians such as Sir Edward Carson used opposition in Ulster (the northeast part of Ireland where Protestants formed a majority) to whip up anti-Catholic and anti-Home Rule feeling. The plan was to destroy Home Rule for all Ireland, but instead it created the demand for a separation of Ulster from the rest of Ireland. In 1912, the Ulster Volunteer Force was formed to create a military force opposed to Home Rule. Some 100,000 Irish unionists planned to defy the British government and in 1914, the UVF received arms from Germany and the potential for major armed conflict rose.

Supporters of Home Rule

In 1913, supporters of Home Rule created the Irish Volunteers and mobilised 200,000 men to defend Home Rule, if necessary by armed might. The Irish Volunteers also received German arms in 1914, but were less heavily armed than the UVF.

4.2 THE THREAT OF CIVIL WAR

By the outbreak of the First World War, Ireland seemed to be on the verge of civil war. The government had failed to find a peaceful compromise and when war broke out the UVF formed the 36th (Ulster) Division of the British army. Large numbers of the 36th Division died on the first day of the Battle of the Somme in 1916. Meanwhile the Irish Volunteers were infiltrated by members of the Irish Republican Brotherhood (IRB).

EXAMINER'S TIP

This topic appears at both AS and A2 in the AQA specification (Alternative Q [Britain 1815–1914] and R [Britain 1895–1951]). At AS you will be expected to explain why the crisis took place or how the Liberals dealt with it. In both cases do not describe but provide reasons to support your answer. At A2 you will be expected to write a balanced, analytical answer. The Ulster Crisis usually appears in a question along with other problems facing the Liberals between 1910 and 1914.

5 How did the Easter Rising of 1916 lead to a major change in British–Irish relations?

5.1 THE EASTER RISING

The Easter Rising was an attempt by a small number of republican revolutionaries to create an Irish republic by violent means. A group of IRB members within the Irish Volunteers, led by Patrick Pearse, attempted to dupe other volunteers into taking part in a rebellion. Approximately 1,200 volunteers took part in a rebellion that lasted 1 week at the end of April 1916. It was based in Dublin. The small numbers involved suggest that Pearse and other leaders knew beforehand that the rebellion would fail and that they hoped to use the failure to gain support for an independent republic.

At the December 1918 general election, the rebel party (now known as Sinn Fein) won 73 seats in Parliament. In January 1919, these MPs united with the Home Rule Party MPs to form the *Dáil Eireann*, an Irish national Parliament and government in Dublin which met in defiance of the British government.

5.2 BRITISH REACTION TO THE EASTER RISING

The Easter Rising took place in the middle of a world war amidst strong indications that it had German links. A German ship masquerading as a neutral vessel was scuttled off Ireland and found to be carrying a large amount of arms and ammunition. Sir Roger Casement, a British civil servant with strong Irish nationalist views, was arrested in Ireland after landing from a German U-boat.

Following the collapse of the Easter Rising, General Maxwell — the British commander in Ireland — introduced martial law and executed 16 nationalist leaders, including Patrick Pearse.

5.3 THE IRISH CONVENTION, 1917–18

The British government created an Irish Conference to discuss Ireland's political future, but Irish Unionists prevented any meaningful discussion about self-government. The failure of the convention increased support for Irish republicanism.

5.4 OTHER BRITISH MEASURES

The release of Republican prisoners, 1917

In a bid to appease Irish-American opinion and secure US support in the First World War, the British government released the Easter Rising prisoners. Republican leaders, including Michael Collins, returned to Ireland to campaign for independence.

Conscription

An attempt to extend military *conscription* to Ireland in 1918 followed the German Spring Offensive when Britain needed as many men as it could get for the Western Front. The move united Irish nationalists and greatly increased support for Irish republicanism as Home Rule MPs left Westminster to lead an anti-conscription campaign.

conscription: compulsory military service which had been introduced in the rest of the United Kingdom in 1916.

This topic appears at A2 in the OCR specification, Unit 5 on Britain and Ireland. You should use the information to identify themes in British–Irish relations between 1798 and 1921.
In AQA Alternative R (1895–1951) this topic is part of one on the Unit 3 course essays.
Use the information covering Ireland from 1885 to 1921 to prepare for this essay.

6. Why was Ireland partitioned in 1920–22?

6.1 BACKGROUND

The creation of *Dáil Eireann* in January 1919 led to the outbreak of the Anglo-Irish War of 1919–21. British military and security forces fought a guerrilla campaign against the

Irish Volunteers, who had been renamed the Irish Republican Army (IRA). Reprisals, political assassinations and ambushes were the main features of the war. By January 1922, Ireland was partitioned into Northern Ireland and the Irish Free State.

6.2 THE GOVERNMENT OF IRELAND ACT, 1920

The British government's first response to the outbreak of the Anglo-Irish War was an Act to create two Irish Home Rule Parliaments. One was based in Belfast within an area named as Northern Ireland. A second was created in Dublin in an area entitled Southern Ireland. The Act came into operation in the north only. In the rest of Ireland, Sinn Fein's victory in local elections and the continuation of the Anglo-Irish War between the British authorities and the IRA prevented the introduction of the Act in 'Southern Ireland'.

6.3 THE ANGLO-IRISH TREATY, 1921

The treaty was signed between the British government and representatives of Sinn Fein and had five main provisions:

- It agreed to set up the Irish Free State as a new state within the British empire. The state was to have dominion status, which meant it had the same constitutional position as Canada, with internal self-government but the British remaining in control of foreign policy. The Irish head of state was King George V.
- For security reasons, Britain kept control of the so-called Treaty Ports of Cork Harbour, Berehaven and Lough Swilly.
- Northern Ireland was given the option to join the Irish Free State but declined.
- A Boundary Commission was established to decide on the boundary between Northern Ireland and the Irish Free State. Lloyd George, the British prime minister, gave Irish delegates the impression that a large amount of Northern Ireland would be given to the Irish Free State with the effect of forcing nearly all of Northern Ireland into a united Irish Free State. In 1925, the Boundary Commission reported and made minor adjustments to the border.

6.4 OPPOSITION TO THE ANGLO-IRISH TREATY

There was considerable opposition to the Anglo-Irish Treaty within the Irish republican movement. The *Dáil* split on the issue. Opponents of the treaty rallied under Eamon de Valera, and Arthur Griffith and Michael Collins led the pro-treaty faction. By the summer of 1922, civil war had broken out in the Irish Free State, with victory going to pro-treaty forces. Michael Collins was killed during this war.

EXAMINER'S TIP

This topic appears at A2 in the OCR specification. You will have to identify themes.
In this section use the information to compare British policy with the 1798–1920 period.
In the AQA Alternative R (1895–1951) the topic forms part of the Unit 3 course essay.
Use the information from the sections covering 1885–1921 to prepare for this topic.

7   *Why did the Northern Ireland Troubles begin in 1968?*

7.1 BACKGROUND, 1922–49

From 1922, the Home Rule statelet of Northern Ireland was dominated by the Protestant

Unionist Party. Northern Ireland's Catholics were closely associated with Irish nationalism and were seen by Unionists as supporters of the Irish Free State.

The Irish Free State became Eire in 1937. This was a *republic* within the British Commonwealth and empire, and the head of state became an elected President. Eire stayed neutral in the Second World War. In 1949, Eire became the Republic of Ireland and left the British Commonwealth.

7.2 NORTHERN IRELAND TROUBLES, 1968–72

Anti-Catholic discrimination

By 1968, Northern Ireland Catholic opposition to discrimination in housing, jobs and voting led to the foundation of a Civil Rights Association. It was inspired by the black civil rights movement in the USA and adopted Martin Luther King's tactics of non-violence. Civil rights marches were attacked by Protestant/Loyalist mobs and attracted considerable publicity.

Protestant unrest

By 1969, Protestants had begun to attack Catholic areas of towns such as Belfast. A riot in Derry City, following the Apprentice Boys' March of August 1969, led to a collapse of law and order across Northern Ireland.

British troops go to Northern Ireland

In 1969, Harold Wilson's Labour government sent British troops into Northern Ireland in a bid to restore the rule of law and to protect Catholic areas from attack. James Callaghan, the home secretary, disbanded the B Specials, a part-time, Protestant-dominated police force disliked by Catholics. However, little else changed and Catholics began to see the British army as defenders of the Northern Irish Unionist government. Support for the IRA grew and IRA terrorists began attacks on the British army.

Internment and direct rule

In 1971, the Northern Ireland government attempted to destroy the IRA by introducing internment without trial. The plan backfired because it greatly increased support for the IRA. In 1972, an illegal civil rights march in Derry City was fired on by the Parachute Regiment and 14 marchers were shot dead. This led to the suspension of the Northern Ireland government and Parliament and the introduction of direct rule from London, whereby Northern Ireland was governed by a secretary of state with a seat in the Cabinet.

GLOSSARY

republic: a country without a monarch as head of state.

EXAMINER'S TIP

This topic appears at A2 in AQA Alternative U (Britain 1929–1997) and is important for Unit 6 1969–1998 on Britain and Ireland. Learn, understand and use historical terms associated with Britain and Ireland in this period, such as 'civil rights movement', 'Unionist' and 'republican'. You will need to use the information in this section to place sources in historical context. It is also important to use different historical interpretations of the issue in your answer.

8 How did British governments try to bring peace to Northern Ireland, 1972–98?

8.1 COERCION

In attempting to defeat the IRA and other republican paramilitary groups, the British security forces used a number of tactics, including the use of informants to help arrest paramilitary members, surveillance towers in border areas to monitor IRA movements, the blocking of unapproved roads between Northern Ireland and the Irish Republic, and cooperating with the Irish Republic's police (*Garda*) and army.

Diplock courts

After internment came to an end in the mid-1970s, the British government created the Diplock courts, which tried those accused of terrorist offences without a jury.

The Prevention of Terrorism Act, 1974

This Act was introduced after the Birmingham pub bombings and gave the police and security forces extensive powers to control the movement of people in and out of Northern Ireland.

The SAS

The British government used the Special Air Service (SAS) on undercover operations to locate and assassinate IRA members. In 1987, the SAS killed most of the East Tyrone Active Service Unit of the IRA at Loughgall.

8.2 POLITICAL SOLUTIONS

The Sunningdale Agreement, 1973

The Conservative government attempted to create a Northern Irish power-sharing executive with representatives from the unionist and nationalist communities. It collapsed with the Ulster Loyalist workers' strike of 1974.

Ulster Convention, 1975–76

After the collapse of power sharing, the Labour government attempted to create political agreement by establishing an elected Convention. The anti-power-sharing groups did well in elections to the Convention and it achieved nothing.

The Anglo-Irish or Hillsborough Agreement, 1985

Margaret Thatcher's Conservative government signed an agreement with the Irish Republic with the aim of increasing cross-border cooperation. (It also aimed to reduce support for Sinn Fein, which had grown as a result of the IRA hunger strikes of 1981–82 when the hunger-striker Bobby Sands was elected an MP.) The Agreement broke new ground in recognising the right of the Irish Republic to be consulted about Northern Ireland, and Anglo-Irish ministerial conferences became a regular feature after 1985.

The Downing Street Declaration, 1993

This was an agreement between John Major's Conservative government and the Irish Republic's government. Britain declared it had no selfish economic or strategic interest in Northern Ireland and that Irish unity was a matter for people on the entire island of Ireland. The Downing Street Declaration failed to produce a political settlement because of the British government's insistence on paramilitary *decommissioning* of weapons before political agreement. Major's government was dependent upon Ulster Unionist support to continue in power.

The Good Friday Agreement, 1998

The Good Friday Agreement led to a change in the constitutions of both the United Kingdom and the Irish Republic, with the Irish Republic giving up the claim to Northern Ireland which was made in Eire's constitution of 1937. The agreement also set up a Northern Ireland Assembly and a power-sharing government to include Sinn Fein representatives. Republican and Loyalist prisoners imprisoned for terrorist offences were released and paramilitary groups agreed to decommission their weapons and maintain a cease-fire. The agreement was backed by referendums in Northern Ireland and the Irish Republic and had US government support.

8.3 Effects of the Good Friday Agreement

- It caused a split in the IRA with the Real and Continuity IRA opposed and continuing to engage in terrorism.
- Decommissioning didn't take place. The IRA declared that it was willing to put its weapons beyond use, but not to surrender them.
- Punishment beatings and shootings between Loyalist paramilitary groups continued.
- Ian Paisley's Democratic Unionist Party opposed the agreement.
- The British reduced the army presence in Northern Ireland.
- The Royal Ulster Constabulary was renamed the Northern Ireland Police Service following the Patten Report.

(1) Why were the Conservatives the dominant political party, 1885–1906?

(2) How successful were the Conservatives in domestic affairs, 1885–92?

(3) Why did Chamberlain support tariff reform and what impact did it have on the Conservative Party?

(4) How successful were the Conservatives in foreign and imperial affairs?

1 Why were the Conservatives the dominant political party, 1885–1906?

1.1 BACKGROUND

The Conservatives formed the government in 1885–86, 1886–92 and 1895–1905. Lord Salisbury was prime minister on three occasions, 1885–86, 1886–92 and 1895–1902, and was succeeded by his relation, A. J. Balfour, from 1902 to 1905.

From 1886, the Conservatives were supported by the Liberal Unionist Party, which comprised those Liberals who had left Gladstone's party because of their opposition to Irish Home Rule. Their leaders were the Marquis of Hartington and Joseph Chamberlain. In 1895, the Liberal Unionists merged with the Conservatives to form the Unionist Party.

1.2 THE MAIN REASONS FOR CONSERVATIVE DOMINANCE

Liberal split over Irish Home Rule

During the debate on Gladstone's First Home Rule Bill in 1886, 96 Liberals crossed the floor of the House of Commons and joined forces with the Conservatives. Although the Liberals formed the government between 1892 and 1895, they were dependent on the support of the Irish Home Rule Party.

Gladstone's retirement in 1894

Gladstone had dominated British Liberalism since 1865 and his retirement left a political vacuum. He was succeeded by Lord Rosebery, who was prime minister until a general election defeat in 1895. His resignation left the Liberals technically leaderless until 1898. Sir Lewis Harcourt acted as unofficial leader and, from 1898, the Liberals were led by Sir Henry Campbell-Bannerman, who only enjoyed a limited authority over the party.

The South African War, 1899–1902

The Liberals split into two factions with the Liberal Imperialists, including Asquith and Grey, supporting the Conservative government's decision to go to war. The pro-Boers were against the war and they included Lloyd George. The Liberal leader Campbell-Bannerman deepened Liberal divisions by his 'methods of barbarism' speech against the use of concentration camps in the war.

Villa Toryism

During the period there was a marked increase in middle-class support for Conservatism with the new suburban commercial interests growing disillusioned with many of the radical causes associated with Liberalism. This trend was increased by the Redistribution of Seats Act, 1885, which gave more seats to the suburbs.

Conservative Party organisation

In 1883, the Conservatives created the Primrose League and attracted a large number of women activists to work for the party. The party also started Conservative Workingmen's clubs, which helped spread party support into traditional Liberal areas. From 1884, the principal political agent was Captain Middleton, who led an effective party organisation.

Imperialism

Imperialism was the dominant political theme of an era when the partition of Africa was taking place and Britain was involved in the South African War. Even the Liberal Party was affected and formed a Liberal League to gather support for imperialism and the empire. However, the Conservatives were most closely associated with support for colonial expansion and defence of the empire.

Working-class Conservatism

A significant portion of the working class voted Conservative and this occurred for various reasons:

- Towns with a strong naval and military element, such as Portsmouth, backed Conservative support of a strong navy and army.
- Anti-Catholic feelings in south Lancashire and Liverpool, resulting from large-scale Irish immigration, stimulated support for the Conservative anti-Home Rule stance.
- Deferential voting meant that domestic servants and rural workers tended to vote the way their employers or social superiors told them.
- Many people opposed Liberal support for licensing reform of public houses and alcohol.

2 How successful were the Conservatives in domestic affairs, 1885–92?

2.1 IRELAND

For more detailed information, see Unit 7 Section 3. The main elements in the Conservative policy of 'killing Home Rule with kindness' were:

- the Land Purchase Acts, 1885 and 1891, which helped landless rural labourers to buy their smallholdings

- the Congested Districts Act, 1890, which gave financial help for the economic development of western Ireland
- the Crimes Act, 1887, when the Irish secretary, A. J. Balfour, introduced imprisonment without trial and broke the Land League's campaign of intimidation against landowners

2.2 LABOUR REFORM

The agricultural and trade depressions of the 1880s led to a rise in unemployment, and in 1887 there was rioting in Trafalgar Square by the unemployed. The Conservative government responded with several Acts.

Housing

The Working Class Dwellings Act, 1885, extended powers of local authorities to remove slums and its provisions were bolstered by the Housing of the Working Class Act, 1890.

Small-scale agriculture

The Labourers' Allotment Act, 1887, allowed labourers to rent allotments of land from local authorities to grow their own vegetables. Similar rights were offered to agricultural labourers in the Smallholdings Act, 1892.

Mines Regulation Act, 1887

This legislation extended government regulation of the mining industry.

2.3 EDUCATION REFORM

The 1891 Education Act abolished school fees in elementary schools and created free state education for the first time.

2.4 LOCAL GOVERNMENT REFORM

The 1888 County Councils Act was mainly the work of Joseph Chamberlain. In creating elected local government for the first time outside towns, it was arguably the period's most important reform. The Act established 62 county councils, directly elected by ratepayers.

EXAMINER'S TIP

This topic appears at AS in the OCR specification and at A2 in the Edexcel and AQA specifications. At AS you might be asked to explain why reforms were introduced or how successful they were. At A2 you should write a balanced, analytical answer which uses factual information to support and sustain argument.

3 Why did Chamberlain support tariff reform and what impact did it have on the Conservative Party?

3.1 BACKGROUND

In September 1903, Chamberlain resigned as colonial secretary to lead a national campaign to convert the Conservative Party and the country to the idea of tariff reform. His aim was to unravel the free trade approach, which had been British economic policy since the 1840s, and to protect British industry from foreign competition by placing import taxes (tariffs) on imported goods. Chamberlain claimed that tariff reform would protect and create thousands of jobs and that the revenue raised from import taxes would help pay for old-age pensions and naval development.

3.2 CHAMBERLAIN ABANDONS FREE TRADE

The local background

Chamberlain represented a west Midlands constituency in an area of iron and steel production and engineering which had suffered badly from foreign competition. Chamberlain wanted to protect employment in his own region.

The international background

Virtually all countries had adopted some form of tariff system by 1903, particularly Britain's main economic rivals in Germany and the USA. All Britain was doing was conforming to the world economic trend.

Empire

Chamberlain wanted to strengthen the British empire and believed it faced major threats from other states such as Russia, France and Germany. In the 1880s and 1890s Chamberlain had attempted, but failed, to bring the empire closer together. At the Imperial Conference of 1887 he supported the idea of an imperial parliament for the whole empire. In the 1897 and 1902 Imperial Conferences he suggested a customs union and increased cooperation in imperial defence. His ideas for tariff reform aimed to make the empire a closer trading unit involving an imperial preference, whereby tariffs were placed on imports from outside the empire.

3.3 EFFECTS OF TARIFF REFORM ON THE CONSERVATIVE PARTY

Opposition from within

Chamberlain failed to forewarn his political colleagues of his campaign for tariff reform and his announcement, in September 1903, was a political bombshell. His colleagues responded with various fears:

- Opponents of Chamberlain said that Britain had grown rich under free trade and had used it to become the most important industrial country.
- Many Conservatives, knowing that Britain was a net importer of food, feared that tariff reform would increase the cost of living.
- The same trade-minded faction pointed out that many of Britain's industries, like coal and textiles, were export orientated.
- Many said that tariff reform would start a trade war, which would result in increased unemployment as British exports faced extra taxes.
- The City of London's banking industry — a major investor in overseas projects — feared that tariff reform might lead to a limitation of British investment abroad.

Conservative splits

Chamberlain's campaign had split the Conservatives into three groups:

- the whole-hoggers, who accepted Chamberlain's tariff reform proposals in their entirety
- the free-fooders, who opposed tariff reform and favoured the continuance of free trade
- the Balfourites, who followed the Conservative leader Balfour and favoured a compromise solution of accepting some of Chamberlain's tariff reform proposals

Opposition from without

The tariff reform issue had the effect of reuniting the Liberal Party and was the most important reason for the heavy Conservative election defeat in 1906.

This topic appears at AS in the OCR specification. It appears at A2 in the Edexcel and AQA specifications. Learn, understand and use historical terms associated with this topic, such as 'tariff reform', 'whole-hogger' and 'free-fooder'. At AS you might be expected to explain why Joseph Chamberlain supported tariff reform or why others opposed the proposal. At A2 you will be expected to write analytical answers. Factual information should be used only to support and sustain argument, not to describe or narrate.

4 How successful were the Conservatives in foreign and imperial affairs?

4.1 BACKGROUND

For more detailed coverage, turn to Unit 9 on British foreign policy, 1890–1914.

4.2 AREAS OF INVOLVEMENT

The Mediterranean Agreement

In 1887, Britain signed international agreements with Italy and Austria-Hungary with the aim of preventing the Russian navy entering the Mediterranean. All three powers planned to work together to prevent this development.

The partition of Africa

Salisbury's government supported the extension of British control and influence in Africa with the following measures:

- In 1887, the Royal Niger Company was created to help establish British control of the Lower Niger valley and establish the British colony of Nigeria.
- The East Africa Company took control of Zanzibar and a large part of east Africa in 1888.
- In 1889, the British South Africa Company was given permission to occupy central Africa in an area which included the modern-day states of Zambia and Zimbabwe.
- In 1890, the Heligoland–Zanzibar Agreement with Germany was signed, giving Heligoland in the North Sea to Germany and bringing German recognition of British control in Uganda, Kenya, Nyasaland (Malawi) and Zanzibar.
- In 1890, Britain signed an agreement with France that confirmed British control of Nigeria.

Venezuela, 1895–99

Britain entered a dispute with Venezuela and the USA over claims to territory in British Guyana, South America. The issue was settled by international arbitration when British claims were upheld in 1889.

China, 1898–1900

Britain responded to the German acquisition of Kiaochow in northern China by taking control of the port of Wei-Hei-Wei. This was leased from China in a 99-year deal, dating from 1898, which was a major extension to Britain's colony in Hong Kong. In 1900, Britain took part in an international force to suppress the Boxer Rebellion against foreign influence in China.

The South African War, 1899–1902

This was a major issue in imperial policy which involved Britain in the biggest armed conflict between the Crimean War and the First World War. British victory in 1902 ensured British dominance of southern Africa and control of the South African gold fields. For more detailed coverage, see Unit 9 on British foreign policy, 1890–1914.

The abandonment of splendid isolation, 1902–06

For more detailed coverage, see Unit 9 on British foreign policy, 1890–1914. The main events were:

- the Anglo–Japanese Alliance, 1902, which was Britain's first military alliance since the Crimean War of 1854–56
- the entente cordiale with France, 1904 — a colonial agreement mainly inspired by mutual fear of Germany
- the First Moroccan Crisis, 1905–06, when Britain supported France against German attempts to stop French influence in Morocco

EXAMINER'S TIP

This topic appears at AS in the OCR specification and at A2 in the Edexcel and AQA specifications. Learn, understand and use historical terms associated with foreign policy, such as 'splendid isolation', 'entente cordiale' and 'imperialism'. At AS you might be asked to explain why imperialism was popular in the period. At A2 you might be asked to analyse the reasons behind British actions in foreign and imperial policy in the period. You might also be asked to explain how far Britain was successful in foreign and imperial policy.

KEY QUESTIONS

(1) How strong was Britain's position in the world in 1890?

(2) What was splendid isolation?

(3) Why did Britain fight the South African War, 1899–1902?

(4) Why did Britain abandon splendid isolation, 1900–07?

(5) Why did Britain go to war with Germany in 1914?

1 How strong was Britain's position in the world in 1890?

1.1 BRITAIN AS A WORLD POWER

Empire

Britain had the world's largest empire which, by 1914, covered a quarter of the world's land surface and contained a third of its population.

Industry and finance

Britain was the world's major industrial country and led the world in coal and textile production. Britain was the global financial capital. The City of London dominated insurance through Lloyd's, shipping through the Baltic Exchange and investment through the Stock Exchange.

Navy

Britain had the largest navy. In 1889, Parliament passed the Naval Defence Act to establish the 'two power standard' with the aim of ensuring that the Royal Navy was larger than the next two largest navies combined, i.e. the French and Russian navies. Britain also possessed the largest merchant navy and was the world centre for shipbuilding.

1.2 THREATS TO BRITISH POWER BY 1890

Industrial threat

Britain's position as the world's major industrial power was threatened by the USA and Germany, which had caught Britain up in the production of iron and steel. Foreign competition was a major concern for politicians and businessmen, and there were calls for replacing free trade with protective tariffs.

Colonial threat

Russia was a contender for influence in Afghanistan and Britain feared a common border between the Russian empire and the British Indian empire. Britain also feared that the Russian navy might gain entry to the Mediterranean through the Dardanelles and Bosphorus Straits. The other main colonial rivalry was with France in Africa, where France had opposed Britain's occupation of Egypt since 1882. Both countries were involved in the partition of Africa (in particular, west Africa) and French naval power was a rival to the British navy in both the Atlantic and the Mediterranean.

EXAMINER'S TIP

This topic appears at AS for OCR and at A2 in the Edexcel and AQA specifications. At AS you might be expected to explain Britain's position in world affairs in 1890. At A2 you will be expected to use the information to support an analysis of British foreign policy from 1890 to 1914.

What was splendid isolation?

2.1 NATIONAL SELF-DEFINITION THROUGH OPPOSITION TO BISMARCK

George Goschen, the first lord of the Admiralty, first referred to Britain's isolation in 1896 when he said: 'Our isolation, if isolation it be, was self-imposed. It arose out of our unwillingness to take part in Bismarck's system. Why are we isolated? We are isolated because we will not promise things which we might be unwilling to perform.'

Splendid isolation meant that Britain did not have a formal military or political alliance with another country. The last time Britain had such an arrangement was during the Crimean War of 1854–56 when Britain was in alliance with France and Turkey.

From 1871 to 1890, Bismarck, the German chancellor, formed political and military alliances with several European states, such as Austria-Hungary, Italy, Russia, Romania and Serbia. This is what Goschen meant by 'Bismarck's system'. Russia and France made a formal military and political alliance in 1894.

Britain was offered associate member status of Bismarck's Triple Alliance in 1889, but the prime minister, Salisbury, refused to join. By the mid-1890s, Britain was the only European Great Power not to be in alliance.

2.2 INTERNATIONAL AGREEMENTS

The lack of an alliance did not mean that Britain would not sign international agreements, though when it did so the agreements were on specific issues.

The West Africa Act, 1885

This Act divided west Africa into separate spheres of influence amongst European nations, including Britain, France, Germany and Portugal.

Mediterranean Agreements, 1887

Britain signed naval agreements with Austria-Hungary and Italy, aiming to prevent the Russian navy entering the Mediterranean.

The Heligoland–Zanzibar Agreement, 1890

In this agreement between Britain and Germany, Britain ceded the North Sea state of Heligoland to Germany in return for British control of the east African island of Zanzibar.

2.3 REASONS TO MAINTAIN SPLENDID ISOLATION

Britain did not want to be part of Europe's political and military alliance system for two main reasons:

- Britain's main interests in the world were outside Europe and its major European interest was maintaining the balance of power.
- Britain's main military defence was the navy and — unlike the other European Great Powers — it had volunteer armed forces and a small army located mainly in India.

EXAMINER'S TIP

This topic appears at AS in the OCR specification and at A2 in the Edexcel and AQA specifications. Learn, understand and use historical terms such as 'splendid isolation'.
At AS you might be asked to explain why Britain followed a policy of splendid isolation.
At A2 a more analytical approach will be required and you might be asked to what extent Britain followed a policy of splendid isolation before 1900.

3 *Why did Britain fight the South African War, 1899–1902?*

3.1 BACKGROUND

The South African or Second Boer War was the largest military conflict in the European partition of Africa. It involved the British empire fighting the two independent Dutch republics of the Orange Free State and the Transvaal.

3.2 LONG-TERM REASONS FOR THE SOUTH AFRICAN WAR

Sea routes

Britain had a strategic interest in the Cape of Good Hope, for it overlooked a key point on the sea route from the Atlantic to the Indian Ocean. Britain's naval command of the south Atlantic and Indian oceans depended on its control of the Cape and this is the main reason why Britain acquired it at the Treaty of Vienna, 1815.

Disputes with Dutch settlers

To maintain control of the region Lord Carnarvon had attempted to confederate southern Africa. In 1877, he created a British confederation of Natal, Cape Colony and the Dutch republic of the Transvaal. It collapsed following the defeat of the Zulus in 1879.

The Transvaal's declaration of independence

Between 1880 and 1881, the Transvaal declared its independence and fought Britain in the First Boer War. The war ended with victory for the Transvaal and considerable confusion about the future relationship of Britain and the Transvaal. The Transvaal thought it was completely independent, but Britain thought it still had suzerainty, i.e. that it remained in control of the Transvaal's foreign policy.

3.3 SHORT-TERM REASONS FOR THE SOUTH AFRICAN WAR

Gold in the Transvaal

The discovery of gold in the Transvaal — initially at Baberton in 1882, with the main reserves found in the Witwatersrand in 1886 — immediately made the region into one of the world's major gold producers. Gold was important because the Gold Standard had established it as the basic currency of international trade.

Cecil Rhodes

The *Cape Colony government* was under the control of Cecil Rhodes and he wanted Britain to dominate southern Africa. He was also after wealth, and from 1889 he received British government approval to take over the part of central Africa which is now Zimbabwe, Zambia and Malawi. His failure to find gold there meant that the Transvaal was the wealthiest state in southern Africa, and Rhodes was determined to control it.

The Jameson raid

In 1895, Rhodes planned a take-over of the Transvaal by organising an uprising amongst British miners in the Transvaal who were known as *uitlanders* (outsiders). Military support was to have come from Rhodes' colleague, Jameson, but the Jameson raid of 1895–96 was a fiasco. Jameson was arrested by the Transvaal government and the episode led to a major deterioration in relations between Britain and the Transvaal.

Joseph Chamberlain

In 1895, Joseph Chamberlain became colonial secretary. He was determined to strengthen the British empire and regarded South Africa as one of the empire's weakest links, where he had a duty to increase British influence and control.

3.4 IMMEDIATE CAUSES OF THE SOUTH AFRICAN WAR

British expansionism

The appointment of Alfred Milner as British high commissioner at the Cape in 1897 installed a man who shared Chamberlain's views and was determined to achieve an increase in British influence through war. The issue he chose was the *uitlander* franchise — he demanded that all British subjects in the Transvaal should have the vote. The failure to reach an agreement on this issue forced the Transvaal and the Orange Free State into war with Britain.

3.5 THE COURSE OF THE WAR

British setbacks

British forces in South Africa were initially led by incompetent generals such as Buller and they were taken by surprise in October 1899 when they were attacked by the Boers. The Boers quickly surrounded the British-held towns of Ladysmith, Mafeking and Kimberley.

A war of attrition

Even though Britain had captured most major towns in the Transvaal and the Orange Free State by 1900, they failed to defeat the Boers. British forces denied Boer guerrillas bases from which to operate, and the Boers adopted guerrilla warfare tactics which were difficult to defeat. British victory only came after the introduction of concentration camps, where Boer women and children were imprisoned.

British victory and the emergence of South Africa

The war ended with the Treaty of Vereeniging, 1902, and the Transvaal and the Orange Free State became British colonies. However, by 1906 both colonies had been given internal self-government and in 1910 the Union of South Africa was created containing Cape Colony, Natal, the Transvaal and Orange Free State. Its government was dominated by the Transvaal Dutch.

EXAMINER'S TIP

This topic appears at AS in the OCR specification. Learn, understand and use historical terms such as 'Boer' and *uitlander* associated with the South African War. At AS you might be asked to explain why the war began or to explain its impact on British imperial policy.

4 *Why did Britain abandon splendid isolation, 1900–07?*

4.1 SOUTH AFRICA

Britain's involvement in the South African War caused resentment in much of Europe. Britain felt isolated and was fortunate that no European country intervened on the side of the Boers.

4.2 GERMANY

The German decision to follow *Weltpolitik* (world politics) meant that from the late 1890s Germany planned to create a large overseas empire. As part of this process it decided to build a world-class navy to rival Britain's. This broke the 'two power standard' and threatened Britain's defences and empire.

4.3 JAPAN

In 1902, Britain signed the Anglo-Japanese Alliance, its first military alliance since the Crimean War. Both parties recognised the special interests of each other in China and Japan's interests in Korea. Each side declared that it would stay neutral if either side was involved in a war with another power, and agreed to enter a war if either side became involved in a war with more than one power.

Japan signed the alliance because it feared Russian influence in Korea and north China. Britain wanted to use the Japanese fleet to protect British interests in the Far East so that the Royal Navy could be re-deployed to the North Sea to meet the German naval threat. Britain stayed neutral in the Russo-Japanese war of 1904–05 and Japan joined Britain in the First World War against Germany and Austria-Hungary.

4.4 FRANCE

In 1904 Britain signed the entente cordiale with France, a colonial agreement where both sides — fearful of German colonial ambition — agreed to end their colonial differences. France recognised Britain's influence in Egypt, and Britain recognised French influence in Morocco.

The First Moroccan Crisis of 1905–06 began as a German attempt to destroy the entente cordiale, and an international conference at Algeciras in 1906 met to discuss German objections to French influence in Morocco. The German plan backfired. Britain and most other representatives supported France. These events had the effect of increasing British suspicions of the Germans and making improved relations with France permanent.

4.5 RUSSIA

The Anglo-Russian Entente of 1907 was a colonial agreement over spheres of influence in Persia (Iran). Even after the agreement, Anglo-Russian relations remained tense because of Afghanistan and *the Straits*.

the Straits: the Dardanelles and Bosphorus Straits joined the Black Sea with the Aegean Sea. Constantinople, capital of the Ottoman empire, was on the Bosphorus.

This topic appears at AS in AQA Alternative R (Britain 1895–1951) and A2 in AQA Alternative Q (Britain 1815–1914) and at A2 in the Edexcel specification. Learn, understand and use historical terms associated with the retreat from splendid isolation, such as '*Weltpolitik*', 'alliance' and 'entente cordiale'. At AS you might be expected to explain how Britain retreated from splendid isolation. At A2 you will be expected to provide more effective analysis in questions such as 'How far was Britain's retreat from splendid isolation between 1900 and 1907 due to a fear of Germany?'

Why did Britain go to war with Germany in 1914?

5.1 THE IMMEDIATE REASON

Britain declared war on Germany on 4 August 1914, because the Germans had invaded Belgium. Britain, along with the other Great Powers, had guaranteed Belgian neutrality in the Treaty of London, 1839.

5.2 SHORT-TERM REASONS

The Crowe Memorandum, 1907

This Foreign Office document by a civil servant warned the foreign secretary that Germany's aggressive foreign policy was a threat to Britain.

The Second Moroccan or Agadir Crisis, 1911

Germany attempted to force France to hand over part of the French Congo by opposing French police action in Morocco. This convinced the British government that Germany was aggressive in foreign policy. Britain regarded German action as a direct threat to France, and Lloyd George, the chancellor of the exchequer, used the *Mansion House speech* to warn Germany. The British Home Fleet in the North Sea was put on action stations.

The Second Anglo-French Naval Agreement, 1912

Following the Agadir Crisis, Britain signed a naval agreement with France whereby it would protect the Channel coasts of both countries in the event of war. In return France agreed to protect the Mediterranean in a deal which would have made it difficult for Britain to stay out of a Franco-German conflict.

5.3 GENERAL REASONS

Britain went to war to prevent Germany defeating France, which would have radically altered the European balance of power. By 1914, Britain feared Germany as a naval and colonial rival whose dominance of the European continent would have posed a serious threat to Britain's overseas empire.

GLOSSARY

Mansion House speech: annual speech to representatives of the City of London by the chancellor of the exchequer. Traditionally, the speech is on economic and financial matters, but in 1911 Lloyd George used it to warn Germany.

EXAMINER'S TIP

This topic appears at AS in AQA Alternative R (Britain 1895–1951) and at A2 in AQA Alternative Q (Britain 1815–1914) and in the Edexcel specification. At AS you might be expected to explain why Britain went to war with Germany in 1914. At A2 a more balanced analysis might be required, such as 'To what extent was Britain's decision to go to war based on the need to defend the European balance of power?'

UNIT 10 The Liberal governments, 1905–15

KEY QUESTIONS

(1) Why did the Liberals win a landslide victory in the general election of January 1906?
(2) Why did the Liberals introduce social and welfare reforms, 1906–14?
(3) How did a crisis develop over the House of Lords, 1909–11?
(4) How serious were the crises facing the Liberal governments, 1910–14?

1 Why did the Liberals win a landslide victory in the general election of January 1906?

1.1 TARIFF REFORM, 1903–06

The main reason for Liberal success in 1906 was tariff reform. It helped unite the party behind free trade and attracted some Conservatives, notably Winston Churchill, to defect to the Liberals. The issue split the Conservative Party into three groups:

- the whole-hoggers, who accepted tariff reform completely
- the free-fooders, who supported free trade
- the Balfourites, who favoured the compromise of accepting limited tariff reform

Tariff reform was controversial because:

- many feared it would lead to a rise in the cost of living
- people thought Britain's economic prosperity depended on free trade
- industries such as textiles and coal feared that a trade war would exclude them from overseas markets

1.2 OTHER ISSUES

The Education Act, 1902

Before tariff reform became an issue, the Liberals united to fight education legislation, which they disliked because government money was directed towards Anglican-run schools.

The Liberal–Labour electoral pact, 1903

This *pact* divided constituencies between the two parties and prevented their fighting each other to split a vote and allow the Conservatives the opportunity of winning. In the 1906 general election, the pact helped swing many seats in south Lancashire and Liverpool away from the Conservatives.

Chinese Slavery, 1904

The use of Chinese labourers — who were forced to work and live in inhuman conditions — in the Transvaal gold mines caused a public outcry, which eroded support for the Conservative government. Viscount Alfred Milner, British administrator of the Orange Free State and the Transvaal, was forced to abandon the use of Chinese slaves.

The MacDonnell devolution crisis, 1905

Sir Antony MacDonnell was a civil servant in the Irish Office. His decision to offer a degree of self-government (devolution) to Ireland caused resentment amongst Irish Unionists and led to the creation of the Ulster Unionist Council.

The first-past-the-post electoral system

The electoral system exaggerated the Liberal victory. The Liberals won 400 seats to the

Conservatives' 156. However, when expressed as a proportion of votes cast, the victory appears much less decisive, for the Liberal vote was 2,727,000 compared to the Conservatives' 2,451,000.

2 Why did the Liberals introduce social and welfare reforms, 1906–14?

2.1 THE REFORMS

Liberal social and welfare reforms fell into five categories:

- for the sick and injured
- for the unemployed
- for children
- for the elderly
- for workers

The Unemployed Workmen Act, 1905

This Act established distress committees to give grants to help provide work for the unemployed.

The Workmen's Compensation Act, 1906

Legislation which forced employers to pay compensation to workmen injured at work through accidents or related illness.

Education (Provision of School Meals) Act, 1906

Legislation to provide free school meals to poor children.

The Trades Disputes Act, 1906

This reversed the Taff Vale decision of 1901 and stopped unions from being charged for loss of earnings by firms during a strike.

The Education (Medical Inspection) Act, 1907

This provided free, compulsory medical inspection for school children in order to identify disease.

The Children's Act, 1908

This Act punished people for allowing children to beg, and forbade the sale of alcohol to children under 5 and tobacco to children under 16. In 1912, it was followed by a system of grants to pay for the medical treatment of children.

The Old Age Pensions Act, 1908

This Act established a non-contributory pension scheme providing 5 shillings (25p) per week for people aged over 70 years.

The Mines Act, 1908

This Act introduced an 8½-hour working day in mines.

The Labour Exchanges Act, 1909

This Act set up a national network of job centres where the unemployed could find out what jobs were available.

The National Insurance Act: Part 1, 1911

A new system of health insurance provided for a payment of 10 shillings (50p) a week for a person who was off work because of illness. This lasted for 26 weeks and was funded by a 6d (2.5p) per week contribution with the employee paying 2d, the employer 2d and the government 2d.

The National Insurance Act: Part 2, 1911

This provided unemployment insurance and was aimed at workers in industries with high levels of unemployment, such as construction, shipbuilding and engineering. The unemployed received 7 shillings (35p) per week for a maximum of 15 weeks.

2.2 REASONS FOR THE REFORMS

Research on poverty

In Victorian Britain people believed poverty was mainly due to idleness, a lack of education and a lack of *thrift*. By 1900, two major social studies had proved these ideas to be largely false. Charles Booth's study of London's poor and Seebohm Rowntree's study of York identified a large body of people who were poor through no fault of their own.

The Royal Commission on the Poor Law, 1906–09

This recommended that local administration of the Poor Law should only continue if there was a major change in local government finance and that, in future, help for the poor should also be a matter for central government.

The South African War, 1899–1902

The Inter-Departmental Committee of Physical Deterioration reported in 1904 that many volunteers for the army in 1899–1902 had to be rejected on grounds of ill health and poor physical development. The conclusion was that if Britain was to have a strong army and navy to defend the empire, then it had to have a healthy population.

National efficiency

Many politicians believed that Britain was about to lose its position as the world's leading industrial and commercial nation. Efficiency was identified as the key to continued prosperity, and unemployment was seen as a waste of labour, which stood in the way of improving Britain's economy.

New Liberalism

There was a feeling that Gladstone's form of liberalism — which believed in minimal government intervention in the economy and society — was out of date. Many early twentieth-century Liberals now thought that the government should intervene to help what they called 'the deserving poor'.

Pressure from outside Parliament

Three examples of external pressure on Parliament are:

- trade unionists who wanted the Taff Vale decision reversed
- the Miners' Federation of Great Britain, which wanted shorter working hours
- children's societies, which wanted greater protection for children

2.3 THE LIBERAL CONTRIBUTION TO FOUNDING THE WELFARE STATE

Liberals had no overall plan for social and welfare reform and many of the above Acts were the result of personal initiatives by individual ministers. For example, Lloyd George was most responsible for pensions legislation and Part 1 of the 1911 National Insurance Act, and Winston Churchill was most responsible for Labour Exchanges.

The Liberals helped create a social service state in which the government provided minimal help for the deserving poor. The undeserving poor were excluded, those receiving Poor Law relief could not get a pension and National Insurance was not open to those who had been dismissed from work.

GLOSSARY

thrift: saving money or spending it wisely.

EXAMINER'S TIP

This topic appears at AS in AQA Alternative R (Britain 1895–1951) and in the Edexcel and OCR specifications. It is an A2 topic in AQA Alternative Q (Britain 1815–1914). Learn, understand and use historical terms associated with Liberal reforms, such as 'deserving poor' and 'social service state'. At AS you might be expected to explain why the Liberals introduced reforms. At A2 you might be expected to provide a balanced, analytical response to questions, such as 'To what extent did the Liberals lay the foundations for a welfare state?' In this answer, you would have to define 'welfare state' and to assess whether or not the Liberals planned such a policy.

3 How did a crisis develop over the House of Lords, 1909–11?

3.1 REASONS FOR LIBERAL CONFLICT WITH THE HOUSE OF LORDS

Long-term reasons

The House of Lords was dominated by Conservatives and when Liberal governments were in power they had the power to reject (veto) legislation, such as the Second Home Rule Bill in 1893. Between 1905 and 1909, the Lords rejected an Educational Bill which would have changed the Education Act, 1902, a Licensing Bill and a plan to value Scottish land.

Immediate reasons

The House of Lords rejected the Liberal 'People's Budget' of 1909, which was designed to raise money to pay for naval building and old age pensions. The Lords objected to progressive taxation proposals which included:
- an increase of income tax by 1p in the pound on incomes over £3,000 per year
- a new super tax of 6d (2.5p) in the pound on incomes over £5,000

- a particularly controversial tax on *unearned increment on land* which hit large landowners, including many members of the House of Lords, who were doubly outraged by suggestions for a land survey to make sure that correct amounts of land tax could be levied
- an increase in death duties
- an increase in tax on property

The Lords rejected the budget by 350 to 75 votes and — as no budget had been voted down like this since the Cavalier parliament of the 1660s — it caused a constitutional crisis.

3.2 THE POLITICAL CRISIS, 1910–11

The crisis was more about the constitution than the budget. The Liberals were determined to end the House of Lords' absolute veto.

The January 1910 general election

Following the rejection of the People's Budget in November 1909, Asquith, the prime minister, called a general election. Though the Liberals received 2.9 million votes (more than in 1906), the Liberal allocation of seats fell from 400 to 272. Nevertheless, the Liberals were supported by 82 Irish Home Rule MPs and 42 Labour MPs. The budget was reintroduced and finally accepted by the House of Lords in April 1910.

Death of King Edward VII

The King's death in May 1910 delayed the opportunity of finding a political solution to the problem. The new king, George V, was politically inexperienced.

The Constitution Conference

In June–November 1910, an attempt was made to forge a compromise between the Liberals and Conservatives with the Liberal Asquith and the Conservative Balfour leading discussions. A party truce was called for during the conference, but no common ground between the two sides could be found.

Lloyd George's secret attempt to find a political solution

Simultaneous with the Constitution Conference, Lloyd George, the Liberal chancellor of the exchequer, met secretly with the Conservatives to find a solution. He suggested the creation of a national government of Conservatives and Liberals, which would introduce compulsory military service (conscription) to please the Conservatives if they accepted 'Home Rule all round' (i.e. for Ireland, Scotland and Wales). Lloyd George's attempt failed because he was the only go-between in the secret negotiations and promised each side something that the other would find unacceptable if the negotiations were made public. He supported the idea of a coalition government because he feared the rise of Germany and believed Britain would be better served by a strong non-party government.

The December 1910 election

Following negotiations with George V, a second election was called and the main issue was reform of the House of Lords. The Liberals won 272 seats (275 in January), the Conservatives 272 (273 in January) and the balance of power was held by the Irish Home Rule Party with 84 seats. The King agreed to create enough peers to ensure reform of the House of Lords.

The Parliament Act, 1911

The Parliament Bill became law when large numbers of Conservative peers refused to vote. The Parliament Act ended the House of Lords right to reject bills. All that was allowed was a delaying veto, giving the Lords the right to hold up a Bill for 2 years if it had passed the House of Commons on three successive occasions. This was sanctioned in the belief that a general election might occur in the 2-year period to allow the electorate the chance to vote on the issue. The Lords lost all rights to discuss 'money bills' which contained a financial element, and the speaker of the House of Commons was given the right to decide what constituted a money bill.

3.3 THE IMPACT OF THE CRISIS

The Parliament Act completely changed the balance of power in Parliament. The House of Commons was now dominant after a process of constitutional change which had begun with the Great Reform Bill crisis of 1832. Since the Parliament Act, it has become a convention (custom) of Parliament that all prime ministers must sit in the House of Commons.

Under the delaying powers of the Parliament Act only two bills were affected — the Home Rule Bill, 1912, and the Welsh Disestablishment Bill, 1912.

GLOSSARY

unearned increment on land: increase in value of land without any attempt physically to improve the land. Land prices rose because of inflation or increased demand for land.

EXAMINER'S TIP

This topic appears at AS in the AQA Alternative R (Britain 1895–1951) and in the Edexcel and OCR specifications. It appears at A2 in AQA Alternative Q (Britain 1815–1914). Learn, understand and use historical terms associated with the conflict with the House of Lords, such as 'budget', 'unearned increment' and 'progressive taxation'. At AS you might be asked to explain why the conflict developed. Alternatively, you might be asked about the consequences of the conflict. At A2 you might be asked to provide a balanced, analytical answer to a question such as 'How far was the conflict between the Liberals and the House of Lords inevitable?'

4 How serious were the crises facing the Liberal governments, 1910–14?

4.1 BACKGROUND

In addition to trouble with the House of Lords, the Liberals faced three other crises in domestic affairs:
- the Ulster Crisis, 1912–14
- the Great Labour Unrest, 1910–14
- the suffragette movement

The Ulster Crisis was the most serious of these and created problems of law and order for the government. Labour unrest caused considerable economic disruption but wasn't a threat to constitutional government. The suffragettes gained considerable publicity but had a limited effect on politics.

In 1935, the historian George Dangerfield published *The Strange Death of Liberal England,* in which he claimed that the Liberals declined as a major party because of the combination of crises prior to 1914.

4.2 CAUSES OF THE ULSTER CRISIS, 1912–14

Long-term causes

There was long-standing opposition to Home Rule in Ireland from Protestants who feared domination by the Catholic majority in a Home Rule Parliament. Others felt that Home Rule would split up the United Kingdom at a time when the British empire faced threats from Germany and other Great Powers, and that Ireland had benefited from the economic links with Britain.

Meanwhile, Sir Edward Carson, a leading Irish opponent of Home Rule, used opposition in northeast Ireland (Ulster — the only area of Ireland where Protestants were in a majority) to try to stop Home Rule.

The immediate cause

The crisis was precipitated by the passage of the Parliament Act, 1911, which prevented the Lords from rejecting a Home Rule Bill. The Irish Home Rule Party held the balance of power in the House of Commons and — in return for support over the Parliament Act — the Liberals introduced a Home Rule Bill.

4.3 HOME RULE OPPOSITION

The Solemn League and Covenant, 1912

A large petition was signed by thousands of Ulster Protestants and presented to Parliament in London. It had no effect on the Liberals.

The Ulster Volunteer Force (UVF), 1912

A military force limited to 100,000 men was formed in Ulster to oppose Home Rule by violence if necessary. Asquith, the prime minister, took no action in case it made matters worse. In 1914, the UVF received arms from Germany and became a major military threat to the government.

Secret negotiations, 1913–14

Meetings between Liberals and Conservatives were organised by Max Aitken, owner of the *Daily Express* newspaper. They were an attempt to reach a compromise but they failed to produce a solution.

4.4 LIBERAL GOVERNMENT ACTION IN ULSTER

Asquith: 'wait and see'

Asquith was noted for the phrase 'wait and see'. He decided to ignore events in Ulster and allow the Home Rule Bill to become law by September 1914. He only acted when forced to by the course of events.

UVF militancy and army acquiescence

Following the UVF's acquisition of arms, Asquith took action. The army was given orders to occupy Ulster in case of violence and the Curragh Incident of 1914 occurred when British army officers with links to Ulster were given the option of not taking part in the plan. A large number of army officers accepted the option.

Churchill deploys the navy

The first lord of the Admiralty, Winston Churchill, moved units of the Royal Navy to Lamlash Bay, in Scotland, as a government threat to the UVF.

The Buckingham Palace Conference

In June–July 1914, George V convened a conference involving the Liberals, Conservatives, Irish Home Rule and Irish Unionist groups. They failed to reach a compromise and the main area of conflict was whether part or all of Ulster should be excluded from Home Rule for a period of time.

4.5 THE SERIOUSNESS OF THE ULSTER CRISIS

The Ulster Crisis came to a temporary halt with the outbreak of the First World War in August 1914 when the UVF joined the British Army as the 36th (Ulster) Division. But the crises ran deep into national life for several reasons:

- The Liberal government faced a well-armed force of 100,000 UVF Protestants who were prepared to resist Home Rule by violence.
- From 1913, an opposing force of 200,000 Catholic Irish Volunteers prepared to defend Home Rule by violence if necessary.
- Asquith's 'wait and see' approach had allowed the crisis to become a serious threat to the government.

4.6 THE GREAT LABOUR UNREST, 1910–14

Britain faced a wave of national strikes involving miners, railwaymen and dockers plus local strikes by seamen, transport and textile workers. Many found evidence to suggest that the government faced a broader political threat from trade unionists and socialists.

Syndicalism

Many workers supported syndicalism, and the syndicalist Tom Mann played an important role in some of the strikes. Syndicalists put forward the view that industrial action could bring down the government and produce a socialist society. An example of this view is to be found in the *Next Step*, a syndicalist pamphlet produced by an unofficial committee of striking Welsh miners in 1911.

The Triple Industrial Alliance

In 1914, the miners, railwaymen and transport workers formed the Triple Industrial Alliance with a declaration that if any one of the three unions went on strike, the other two would follow. Meanwhile, unions began to merge to form large groupings such as the National Union of Railwaymen.

Reasons for strikes

There were three main reasons for the Great Labour Unrest in the run-up to the First World War:

- a rise in the cost of living during a period of near full employment and inflation, both of which fuelled demands for wage rises
- disillusionment with national union officials and a growing gap between local and national control, with many local officials calling strikes
- disillusionment with a Labour Party which had failed to defend trade union interests effectively in Parliament

4.7 THE SUFFRAGETTES
Tactics

The suffragettes received considerable publicity for attacking politicians including the prime minister, setting fire to pillar boxes, chaining themselves to railings in public places and defacing paintings in the National Gallery. In 1913, Emily Davison committed suicide by throwing herself under the King's horse in the Epsom Derby.

Support

The suffragettes had limited support. The government introduced the Cat and Mouse Act, 1913, to defuse the problem of suffragette hunger strikers in prison. They were released when they started a hunger strike and re-arrested once they had eaten.

suffrage: the right to vote.

This topic appears at AS in AQA Alternative R (Britain 1895–1951) and in the Edexcel and OCR specifications. It appears at A2 in AQA Alternative Q (Britain 1815–1914). Learn, understand and use historical terms associated with this period, such as 'syndicalism', 'suffragette' and 'Unionist'. At AS you might be asked to explain why 1910–14 was a period of political and social unrest. At A2 you will be expected to provide an analytical answer to questions such as 'How serious a threat was the social and political unrest in the period 1910–14 to Britain's political stability?'

(1) Why had independent Labour political groups formed by the 1890s?
(2) Why was the Labour Representation Committee (LRC) created in 1900 and how had it developed by 1906?
(3) How effective was the Labour Party in Parliament, 1906–14?
(4) What impact did the First World War have on the rise of the Labour Party?
(5) How effective were the two Labour governments of 1924 and 1929–31?
(6) Did Ramsay MacDonald betray the Labour Party in August 1931?

1 Why had independent Labour political groups formed by the 1890s?

1.1 AN EMERGING CRITIQUE OF CAPITALISM

From the 1850s to the 1880s, most trade unionists supported the Liberal Party and ideas of meritocracy. In 1874, two Liberal/Labour working-class MPs were elected: Thomas Burt and Alexander Mcdonald.

By the 1890s, Britain had become industrialised and large numbers of people lived in towns and worked in manufacturing. This industrial working class faced poor housing and working conditions and had come to look to trade unions for support. Meanwhile, many political and economic writers had begun to criticise the social and economic system that had brought industrialisation. Capitalism was criticised for creating a great imbalance in economic wealth, and writers such as Karl Marx wanted to see the capitalist system replaced by socialism — a social and economic system based on equality in the distribution of wealth. Other writers believed that socialism was the type of society most closely associated with the views of Jesus Christ and there was a division between Marxists and Christian socialists.

1.2 THE MAIN LABOUR GROUPS

By the early 1890s, a variety of Labour political groups had formed.

The Fabian Society

The Fabians were formed in 1883 by middle-class intellectuals who believed they could convince politicians and policy makers to introduce socialism by the strength of argument. They believed that a shift towards socialism could be a peaceful, gradual process.

The Social Democratic Federation (SDF)

The SDF was founded in 1884 by H. Hyndman, a wealthy Marxist who supported a complete social and economic transformation of society.

The Independent Labour Party (ILP)

The ILP began in Bradford during 1893 and was a mixture of Fabians, trade unionists, labour clubs and members of the SDF who supported the collective ownership of the economy.

This topic appears at AS in the OCR specification and at AS and A2 in the AQA specification. Learn, understand and use historical terms associated with the foundation of the Labour Party such as 'Marxist', 'Fabian' and 'ILP'. At AS you might be asked to explain why independent Labour political groups were formed. At A2 you might be asked to explain what was the most important reason for the development of independent Labour political groups.

2 Why was the Labour Representation Committee (LRC) created in 1900 and how had it developed by 1906?

2.1 EARLY DAYS

The LRC was formed in 1900 as a result of trade union action prompted by a number of other factors.

Liberal decline

The Liberal Party split in two after the introduction of the First Home Rule Bill. A traditional Liberal support of workers' interests had waned to the extent that the belief that it would choose working-class parliamentary candidates had virtually disappeared.

Employers' hostility

In the 1890s, trade unions faced a major attack from employers who were supported by court judgements that underlined the lack of working-class political influence.

The Trades Union Congress, 1899

At the Trades Union Congress of 1899, the Amalgamated Society of Railway Servants called for a conference to meet to discuss labour representation in Parliament. The conference met in 1900 and was attended by Fabians, SDF members, the Independent Labour Party and some trade unions. They decided to set up the LRC to fight for trade union and workers' rights in Parliament, and in the 1900 general election the LRC returned two MPs to Parliament.

2.2 DEVELOPMENTS, 1900–06

Taff Vale, 1901

The LRC received a boost to its membership with the Taff Vale decision of 1901 when a court decision made trade unions liable to compensate employers for any losses incurred during a strike. Associated membership of the LRC rose to 850,000 by 1903 after 168 trade unions *affiliated* to the LRC and agreed to finance the effort to get the court ruling amended.

The Lib–Lab pact, 1903

The Liberal Herbert Gladstone (William Gladstone's son) and the LRC's Ramsay MacDonald made an agreement to prevent a conflict between Liberal and Labour candidates. The two parties agreed to split constituencies between them and the pact gave the LRC a free run against the Conservatives in a number of constituencies. In the January 1906 election, the LRC won working-class Liverpool and south Lancashire seats from the Conservatives.

The January 1906 general election

In the January 1906 election, the LRC won 29 seats and gained 5.9% of the vote. After the election, the victorious MPs agreed to re-christen the LRC as the Labour Party.

affiliated: linked to.

This topic appears at AS in the OCR specification and at AS and A2 in the AQA specification. It is AS in AQA Alternative R (Britain 1896–1951) and A2 in Alternative Q (Britain 1814–1914). At AS you might be asked to explain why the Labour Representation Committee was founded. At A2 you might be expected to compare one reason against others in questions such as 'How far was disillusionment with the Liberal Party the reason why trade unions formed the LRC in 1900?'

3 How effective was the Labour Party in Parliament, 1906–14?

3.1 BACKGROUND

Between 1906 and 1914, the Labour Party fought three general elections. While its share of the vote rose from 5.9 % in 1906 to 7.1 % in December 1910, its number of seats rose more sharply from 29 in 1906 to 42 in December 1910.

3.2 MAIN EVENTS

The Trades Disputes Act, 1906

In 1906, the Liberal government withdrew its bill to change the trade union law which was affected by the 1901 Taff Vale decision. Instead, a Labour *private member's bill* was accepted. It became the Trades Disputes Act, 1906, and removed trade unions from any liability for damages caused by a strike.

Trade depression, 1907–08

The Labour Party was affected by the trade depression of 1907–08. Independent socialists won by-elections in this period.

New Liberalism

The Labour Party was adversely affected by the growth of New Liberalism, a view which copied Labour policy by supporting the idea of government intervention to help the poor. It led to the introduction of old age pensions in 1908 and National Insurance in 1911. In 1914, the chancellor of the exchequer, Lloyd George, launched a Land Campaign to nationalise land.

The People's Budget, 1910

The acceptance of the People's Budget in 1910 established the principle of progressive taxation, thus attracting working-class support back to the Liberals. As British politics was becoming class-based, there seemed little room for the Labour Party.

Affiliation with the miners and payment for MPs

In 1908, the Miners' Federation of Great Britain became affiliated to the Labour Party. This was a significant shift away from the Liberal Party which helped swing important mining constituencies towards Labour. In 1911, the introduction of payment for MPs helped working-class people stand for Parliament.

Trade Union Amendment Act, 1913

This Act reversed the 1909 Osborne Judgement and allowed trade unions to raise a political levy from their members in support of the Labour Party. Individual trade union members could opt out of the political levy.

3.3 THE POSITION IN 1914

In local government, the Labour Party won control of London County Council. However, the *Parliamentary Labour Party* was divided between union-sponsored MPs and supporters of the party secretary, Ramsay MacDonald. He wanted to give general support to the Liberal Party, whereas the ILP MPs wanted to judge each Liberal measure on its merits. The historian, Roy Douglas, has pointed out that if anyone in 1914 had said Labour would form a government within 10 years, they would have been ridiculed. Labour had launched the *Daily Sketch* national newspaper by 1914.

GLOSSARY

Parliamentary Labour Party: Labour MPs and the small number of Labour peers in the House of Lords.
private member's bill: a proposal for a change in the law made by a backbench MP, as opposed to a government-sponsored public bill.

EXAMINER'S TIP

This topic appears at AS in the OCR specification. It appears at AS and A2 in the AQA specification. Learn, understand and use historical terms associated with the early history of the Labour Party, such as the 'Taff Vale decision' and 'Parliamentary Labour Party'. At AS you might be expected to explain how the Labour Party developed between 1906 and 1914. At A2 you might be asked to what extent the Labour Party had established itself as a political force by 1914.

4 What impact did the First World War have on the rise of the Labour Party?

4.1 THE SPLIT IN THE LIBERAL PARTY

The Liberals were Labour's main rival for the working-class vote. In 1914, the Liberals had won three successive general elections and seemed to be Britain's natural governing party. In December 1916, Asquith resigned as prime minister to be replaced by Lloyd George, another Liberal. The change of leadership split the party into National Liberal (Lloyd George) and Asquithian factions. The rift widened after the Maurice Debate in 1918 when General Maurice accused the government of stinting on supplies to meet the German Spring Offensive. In the December 1918 general election, the Liberal factions fought against each other.

4.2 THE UNION OF DEMOCRATIC CONTROL

This pressure group was set up by E. D. Morel, a Liberal who favoured public disclosure of international treaties and military alliances in the belief that the First World War would not have taken place had the people of the combatant nations been aware of the secret military commitments their leaders had made. The Union attracted Liberal supporters disillusioned with the Liberal government's secret naval commitments to France before 1914. The Labour Party already supported democratic control of foreign policy and this meant that many Liberals switched their support to Labour.

4.3 LABOUR LEAVES THE NATIONAL COALITION

Arthur Henderson resigned as Labour Party representative in the Lloyd George national coalition government because he was refused permission to attend a socialist conference in neutral Sweden to discuss ways of ending the First World War. Henderson spent 1917–18 reorganising the Labour Party and, with the help of Sidney Webb, he produced a new party constitution. This committed the Labour Party to socialist ideas such as the common ownership of land and the economy, and broadened the membership base by allowing individuals to join the party directly without belonging to an affiliated trade union.

4.4 THE 1918 GENERAL ELECTION

By 1918, the British party system offered the electorate a choice of Conservative, Labour and two Liberal parties. In the 1918 general election, the Labour Party was in a position to fight an effective campaign and its vote rose to 22.2%, with 2.2 million votes and 63 seats.

EXAMINER'S TIP

This topic appears at AS in the AQA and OCR specifications. Material in this section could be used in the Edexcel A2 unit on the Decline of the Liberal Party. Learn, understand and use historical terms associated with this period, such as 'Union of Democratic Control', 'coalition government' and 'constitution'. At AS you might be asked to explain how the First World War affected the development of the Labour Party. At A2 you will be expected to produce a more balanced analysis and, for example, judge the extent to which the rise of Labour between 1914 and 1918 led to the decline of the Liberal Party. At A2 it is important to be aware of and use different historical interpretations.

5 How effective were the two Labour governments of 1924 and 1929–31?

5.1 MINORITY GOVERNMENTS

The first two Labour governments were minority governments where Labour depended on the support of the Liberal Party. Between 1918 and 1924, the Labour Party was successful in winning support from the new electorate created by the Reform Act of 1918. By the January 1924 general election, Labour was the second largest party in Britain, having gained 30.5% of the vote and 191 seats. Although in power for a relatively short period of time, the Labour governments made significant changes in domestic and foreign and imperial policy.

5.2 THE FIRST LABOUR GOVERNMENT, 1924

Domestic affairs

Clifford Allen, leader of the *Independent Labour Party*, wanted the Labour government to introduce radical social measures and then go to the country, in a general election, to gain endorsement. The prime minister, Ramsay MacDonald, preferred a more cautious route and wanted to show that he could govern in the national interest, not just for the trade unions and the working class. His most radical policy was Wheatley's Housing Act. This gave central government money to local authorities to build houses for rent and continued the housing policy of Christopher Addison, the minister of health in Lloyd George's coalition government. With unemployment, Labour did little beyond funding public works schemes, and MacDonald refused to get involved in strikes by the dockers and London transport workers.

Foreign and imperial affairs

Labour's recognition of the USSR and attempts to provide it with loans caused criticism, and the publication of the Zinoviev Letter in the press, suggesting that the Communists planned to overthrow the government, caused a sensation.

MacDonald attempted to increase the authority of the League of Nations and signed the Geneva Protocol, which promised to accept peaceful settlement of international disputes and to disarm by agreement.

In Europe, MacDonald chaired the London Conference, which produced the Dawes Plan to help Germany pay reparations and bring an end to the Franco-Belgian occupation of the Ruhr industrial region of Germany.

Within the empire, work was halted on building a naval base at Singapore.

5.3 THE SECOND LABOUR GOVERNMENT, 1929–31

Domestic affairs

In 1929, there was rising unemployment and Philip Snowden, the chancellor of the exchequer, refused any major intervention and took a cautious view towards government spending. The more radical Sir Oswald Mosley wanted the Labour government to introduce radical social reforms, public works schemes and industrial protection. The failure of MacDonald to accept Mosley's advice led to the latter's resignation from Labour and the formation of the New Party, which subsequently became the British Union of Fascists.

Labour faced financial and political crises following the May Committee Report which predicted a budget deficit of £120 million and called for a £96 million cut in public expenditure. This would have slashed unemployment benefit and the Cabinet would only agree to a £56 million cut. In August 1931, MacDonald decided to form a national government containing Labour, Liberal and Conservative representatives. His decision split the Labour Party.

Foreign and imperial affairs

The Round Table Conference on India, 1930, discussed increasing Indian self-government following the 1929 Simon Commission Report on India and a civil disobedience campaign led by Ghandi and Nehru. Other foreign policy events included:
- the removal of British troops from the Rhineland, 1930
- the recognition of Iraqi independence, 1930
- the evacuation of British troops from Wei-Hei-Wei in northern China, 1930
- a white paper by Lord Passfield (Sidney Webb), the colonial secretary, suggesting decreased Jewish immigration to Palestine, 1930

Independent Labour Party (ILP): a group within the Labour Party founded in 1893 as a socialist faction in favour of a radical transformation of society and politics.

This topic appears at AS in the OCR and at AS in AQA Alternative U (Britain 1929–1997). It appears at A2 in AQA Alternative R (Britain 1895–1951). Learn, understand and use historical terms associated with the Labour governments, such as 'minority government', 'the May Committee' and 'ILP'. At AS you might be asked to explain what changes the Labour Party made in government or to assess Labour Party success. At A2 a more balanced, analytical approach will be required. You might be asked to analyse how radical the Labour governments were. In this question you would be expected to define the word 'radical'. Remember, there are different historical interpretations of the performance of the Labour governments.

6 Did Ramsay MacDonald betray the Labour Party in August 1931?

6.1 THE COALITION

After rising unemployment and the May Committee's recommendation for cuts in public expenditure, Ramsay MacDonald formed a coalition government.

6.2 THE CASE AGAINST MACDONALD'S BETRAYAL

- MacDonald was one of Labour's most experienced and effective leaders. Between 1911 and 1914 he was party secretary, and after the First World War his moderate approach won voters over to the Labour Party.
- In the first Labour government he helped transform Labour from a party of protest into a party of government. He increased Labour's international prestige at the London Conference on Germany and over the Geneva Protocol.
- In August 1931, he had little choice but to form a coalition government. Economic advice from the Treasury and the City of London suggested that cutting public expenditure was the only option facing the government. Although economists such as Keynes and politicians such as Mosley suggested otherwise, their views were very much in the minority. At the time, all governments in the western world were attempting to cut public expenditure.
- The Labour Cabinet agreed that cuts should be made and only differed from MacDonald on the degree of the cuts.
- MacDonald believed a national government was required because Britain faced a major national emergency and he thought it would last a relatively short time. Once the crisis was over, then normal politics would return. As events turned out, the national government lasted until 1945.

6.3 THE CASE FOR MACDONALD'S BETRAYAL

- MacDonald was obsessed with trying to prove that a Labour government put national interests first and his moderation was so pronounced that it went against assisting the very people the Labour Party was created to help: the poor and unemployed.

- MacDonald failed to consult his colleagues adequately and tended to heed advice from the civil service and bankers. He didn't listen to the representatives of the Trades Union Congress or the Labour Party.
- MacDonald's lack of consultation led to a split in his own party when the national government was announced. Most *rank and file* members of the *Parliamentary Labour Party* (PLP) opposed MacDonald's decision.
- The split in the Labour Party undermined its performance in the 1931 general election when Macdonald's National Labour won 13 seats with only 1.6% of the vote. The Labour Party, in opposition to MacDonald, won 56 seats and 30.6% of the vote. Compare that performance to the 288 seats won in the 1929 general election.

GLOSSARY

Parliamentary Labour Party: Labour MPs and the small number of Labour peers in the House of Lords.
rank and file: Labour MPs who were not members of the Labour government.

EXAMINER'S TIP

This topic appears at AS in the OCR specification and at AS and A2 in the AQA specification. It is an AS topic in AQA Alternative U (Britain 1929–1997) and A2 in AQA Alternative R (Britain 1895–1951). At AS you might be asked why Ramsay MacDonald formed the national government in August 1931. At A2 you might have to analyse whether MacDonald was the 'Great Betrayer of his Party'. In answering this type of question, remember that the issue is open to different historical interpretations.

KEY QUESTIONS

(1) How strong was the Liberal Party in 1914?
(2) How did the outbreak of the First World War affect the Liberal Party?
(3) How important was the split between Asquith and Lloyd George in the decline of the Liberals?
(4) Why did Lloyd George fall from power in October 1922?
(5) Did Asquith miss an opportunity for revival in January 1924?
(6) How far had the Liberals declined by 1931?

1 How strong was the Liberal Party in 1914?

1.1 LIBERAL SUCCESS

By 1914, the Liberals had won three successive general elections in 1906, in January 1910 and in December 1910. Against this background of success most Liberals were confident they would win the general election which was likely to take place in 1915.

1.2 REASONS FOR LIBERAL CONFIDENCE

Class-based politics

By 1914, Liberal support for progressive taxation, which had been underlined by the People's Budget, was winning support from the working class. The Conservatives supported tariff reform, a set of import taxes supported by the upper classes partly because it spread the tax burden across all taxpayers.

Support from the Irish Home Rule Party

With an average of 80 parliamentary seats, the Irish Home Rule Party held the balance of power in the House of Commons after 1910. They supported the Liberals' introduction of the Irish Home Rule Bill in 1912.

Splits in the Labour Party

As long as Liberals passed social and welfare reforms, the Labour Party could make little impact in the House of Commons. Union-sponsored Labour MPs wanted to give general support to the Liberal government, while the Independent Labour Party (ILP) MPs wanted to judge each piece of Liberal legislation on its merits.

1.3 PROBLEMS SUGGESTING AN IMMINENT LIBERAL DECLINE

Attitude of the miners

The Miners' Federation of Great Britain (MFGB) left the Liberal Party in 1908 and transferred its support — including the ability to influence the vote in mining constituencies — to Labour.

Local government defeats

The London County Council — the largest local government council in the country — went to Labour in 1914.

Publicity

By 1914, the Labour Party had its own national newspaper, the *Daily Sketch*.

This topic appears at A2 in both the Edexcel and AQA specifications. You will be expected to provide analytical answers to questions where factual knowledge is used to support and sustain argument. If you have to analyse sources, use factual knowledge to place the sources in historical context.

2 How did the outbreak of the First World War affect the Liberal Party?

2.1 PARTY SPLITS

The decision to go to war caused a minor division in government ranks with the president of the Local Government Board, John Burns, and two junior ministers resigning. More important was that Liberals were ill-suited to fight a world war because they had traditionally opposed compulsory military service (conscription) and large-scale expenditure on the armed forces. They also tended to oppose extensive government intervention in the economy.

2.2 THE WARTIME COALITION

In May 1915, Asquith, the prime minister, formed a coalition government with the Conservatives, and the Liberals had to accept greater government involvement in the economy. For example, the coalition government created a Ministry of Munitions, under David Lloyd George, to take responsibility for the production of armaments.

This topic appears at A2 in both the AQA and Edexcel specifications. You might be asked to produce a balanced, analytical answer to questions such as 'To what extent was the decline of the Liberal Party due to the First World War?' If so, you will have to compare the impact of the First World War against other factors, such as the rise of Labour and the role of individuals.

3 How important was the split between Asquith and Lloyd George in the decline of the Liberals?

3.1 THE RISE OF LLOYD GEORGE

Asquith was unsuited to the role of wartime prime minister in that he allowed military leaders to make military decisions without much political input from the government. He took time to realise the importance of organising the entire economy and government for all-out war. On the other hand, Lloyd George had developed a reputation for getting things done. He could claim credit for the introduction of old age pensions and National Health Insurance and he had intervened personally to end the 1912 miners' strike. From 1915, Lloyd George achieved a national reputation for organising the munitions industry.

3.2 Lloyd George in power

In December 1916, Lloyd George's suggestion for a smaller Cabinet to conduct the war led to Asquith's resignation and the creation of a new coalition government. Lloyd George — at the cost of a Liberal Party split — took charge and created the Cabinet he desired. He subsequently won praise for organising the British war effort more effectively.

In May 1918, the Maurice Debate in the House of Commons had Lloyd George's government accused of not sending sufficient reinforcements to stop the German Spring Offensive of 1918. The debate was significant because it led to a confrontation between Asquith and Lloyd George, which solidified Liberal differences to the point that the December 1918 election saw Asquithian Liberals fighting Lloyd George Liberals. Lloyd George then attempted to form a *Fusion* Party, comprising his own Liberal supporters and Conservatives. Its aim was to provide an anti-socialist party which would resist the rise of the Labour Party.

4 Why did Lloyd George fall from power in October 1922?

4.1 Postwar success

Lloyd George was acclaimed as the prime minister who won the First World War and he was one of the main negotiators at the Paris Peace Conference along with President Wilson of the USA and Clemenceau of France.

In the December 1918 general election (the Coupon Election), Lloyd George's coalition won 478 seats, with his Liberal Group winning 133 of them. In opposition Asquith won only 28 seats, but the voting discrepancy was far narrower with the Lloyd George faction claiming only 13.5% of the vote compared to 12.1% for the Asquithians. The largest political group was the coalition Conservatives with 335 seats and 32.6% of the vote.

4.2 Lloyd George loses office

Lloyd George was forced from power in 1922 and never held political office again. There were several reasons for this reversal of fortune.

The revival of peacetime politics

The postwar coalition collapsed when the Conservatives quit in 1922, after a backbench revolt centred at the Carlton Club. This led to a general election and, under the new leadership of Andrew Bonar Law, the Conservatives won 345 seats with 38.2% of the vote. Lloyd George's National Liberals won 62 seats with 11.6% of the vote and Labour increased its vote to 29.5% to claim 142 seats.

The Chanak incident

In October 1922, Lloyd George involved Britain in a conflict when the Turks under Kemal Ataturk attacked the town of Chanak in the international zone. Under the 1920 Treaty of Sèvres between the Allies and Turkey, the Dardanelles and the Bosphorus Straits were placed under international control and Lloyd George wanted to prevent the Turks taking them. He was opposed by the Conservatives and the prime ministers of the Dominions.

The creation of the Irish Free State

Many Conservatives criticised Lloyd George for signing the Anglo-Irish Treaty with Sinn Fein in December 1921. This went further than Home Rule by creating an Irish Free State which was part of the empire.

4.3 THE FALL FROM GRACE

Lloyd George's style of government

Lloyd George's approach caused unease and he was accused of acting like a president and of being too reliant on the small group of advisers known as the Downing Street Garden Suburb.

The honours scandal

Lloyd George sold honours to raise money. When a South African financier, Joseph Robinson, was knighted in 1922 there was a Commons debate ripe with accusations that Lloyd George's government was corrupt and sleaze-ridden.

5 | Did Asquith miss an opportunity for revival in January 1924?

5.1 THE 1923 GENERAL ELECTION

In December 1923, the Conservative prime minister Stanley Baldwin called a general election and used the abandonment of free trade as part of his platform. This had the effect of uniting the two wings of the Liberal Party against *economic protection,* and the Liberals campaigned under Asquith, who was their first undisputed leader since December 1916. Asquith even gathered the support of Lloyd George's electoral fund.

5.2 ASQUITH'S FAILURE

The 1924 general election resulted in a three-way split between Conservatives, Liberals and Labour — the Liberals won 159 seats with 29.6% of the vote, the Conservatives won 258 seats with 38.1% of the vote and Labour won 191 seats with 30.6% of the vote. Baldwin resigned and MacDonald, the Labour leader, was asked to form a government with Asquith's Liberals agreeing to give him support. In *A Stranger Death of Liberal England,* the historian Chris Cook questioned Asquith's inability to force MacDonald into a coalition.

Asquith also failed to get MacDonald to introduce a proportional representation system which would have guaranteed the Liberals a sizeable number of seats. Study the seats/votes statistics above to see how the first-past-the-post single majority system of voting led to disparities between the number of votes cast and the seats won.

5.3 A SPEEDY LIBERAL DECLINE

Between January and December 1924 the Liberals kept Labour in power. Though they had minimal influence over government policy, they shared blame with Labour for any problems. In the December 1924 election, the Liberal vote dropped to 17.6% and they won only 40 seats.

GLOSSARY

economic protection: introducing import taxes and abandoning free trade.

EXAMINER'S TIP

This topic appears at A2 in both the AQA and Edexcel specifications, where you might be expected to explain Asquith's role in the decline of the Liberal Party. Edexcel Unit 6 on the Decline of the Liberal Party might ask you to compare Asquith's role with other reasons for the decline of the Liberals. If you have to analyse sources, use the information in this section to place sources in historical context.

6 | *How far had the Liberals declined by 1931?*

6.1 THE 1929 GENERAL ELECTION

The Liberal Party went into the 1929 general election with *The Yellow Book*, a plan to end economic stagnation which had been heavily influenced by the Liberal economist John Maynard Keynes. Asquith had died in 1928 and the party was united under Lloyd George but only won 59 seats with 23.4% of the vote.

As in January 1924, the Liberals supported but did not join a minority Labour government. By keeping Labour in power between 1929 and 1931, the Liberals were badly affected by Labour's inability to deal with unemployment, and Prime Minister MacDonald's decision to form a national government served to split the Liberal Party as severely as it did Labour.

6.2 THE 1931 GENERAL ELECTION

The 1931 election resulted in a three-way split in the Liberal Party:
- the National Liberals, who supported the creation of a national government, won 35 seats with 3.7% of the vote

- the Liberal Party won 33 seats with 6.5% of the vote
- the Independent Liberals won 4 seats with 0.5% of the vote

6.3 AFTER 1931

The Liberal Party never recovered from its electoral defeats and in 1935 its vote fell to 6.4% with 21 seats. The Liberals remained strong in local government in areas such as the West Country.

EXAMINER'S TIP

This topic appears at A2 in both the AQA and Edexcel specifications. You will be expected to answer questions which require analysis. Factual knowledge should be used to support and sustain argument, not merely to describe events. If you have to provide an overall assessment of the reasons for the decline of the Liberal Party, explain and place reasons in order of importance. Remember that the reasons for decline are open to different historical interpretations.

(1) Why did the Conservatives dominate politics between the wars?
(2) Why did the General Strike take place and why did it fail?
(3) How great was the problem of unemployment in Britain in the 1930s?
(4) What did the national government do to try to end the Depression?

1   Why did the Conservatives dominate politics between the wars?

1.1 CONSERVATIVE SUCCESS

The Conservatives held office during 1922–24 and 1924–29 and formed the largest party in the Lloyd George coalition of 1918–22 and the national government of 1931–45.

1.2 REASONS FOR CONSERVATIVE DOMINANCE

Opposition weakness

The Liberal Party was in electoral decline from 1918 onwards and by 1931 had divided into three factions.

Although Labour rose in popularity between 1918 and 1929, the progressive vote was divided between Labour and Liberal parties. Labour formed two minority governments (with Liberal support) in 1924 and 1929–31. In August 1931, Ramsay MacDonald, the Labour prime minister, formed a national government. This split the Labour Party to the extent that it performed badly in the 1931 general election and took nearly the whole of the 1930s to recover.

The electoral system after 1918

From 1918 constituency boundaries were redrawn. The suburbs received more seats and this also benefited the Conservatives. By 1928, men and women over 21 had the right to vote. However, plural voting and university seats still existed and these also benefited the Conservatives.

The creation of the Irish Free State in 1922 removed a large number of Irish MPs who were traditionally anti-Conservative.

Conservative policies

Much of the electorate feared socialism and communism. Stanley Baldwin, the most successful interwar Conservative leader, worked under the maxim of 'safety first' and personified respect of private property and business, and careful financial management. However, the Conservatives also supported moderate social reform, and Neville Chamberlain's health reforms of the late 1920s laid the foundations for the National Health Service after the Second World War.

In foreign affairs the Conservatives had the reputation of defending British interests and spending on a strong defence force to protect the British empire.

Party organisation

The Conservatives had an organisation in all types of constituency and a network of workingmen's clubs ensured support throughout Britain. The party developed a feel for publicity and used newsreels, radio broadcasts and — in the elections of the 1930s — cinema vans. Conservatives could also rely on favourable coverage from the national press in daily newspapers — the *Telegraph, Express, Mail* and *The Times.*

Following the 1929 election defeat, the Conservative Research Department was set up to gather information, draft speeches and generally boost the party's presence.

Effective leadership
The party had strong leaders in Stanley Baldwin (1923–37) and Neville Chamberlain (1937–40).

2 Why did the General Strike take place and why did it fail?

2.1 CAUSES OF THE GENERAL STRIKE, 1926
Unemployment and the growth of trade unions
Following the end of the First World War, Britain faced unemployment problems in its *staple industries,* including shipbuilding, textile and coal. By this time, trade union membership had risen considerably and internal organisation of the labour movement saw a system of locally elected shop stewards.

The coal miners' strike
Coal was Britain's most important staple industry, both as the main energy source and as a major export. The coal mines had been taken into public ownership (nationalised) during the First World War and then returned to private ownership afterwards. However, miners' wages were still *subsidised* by the government.

In June 1925, the mine owners announced a plan to cut miners' wages. TUC support for the miners led the Conservative government to back down from a major industrial confrontation. This was called Red Friday. The government set up the Samuel *Commission* to investigate the mining industry and also announced that the miners' wage subsidy would continue for a further 9 months.

The Samuel Commission reported in March 1926 with suggestions for a long-term reorganisation of the coal industry and for wage cuts. In reply the miners asked for TUC support in a General Strike and workers in most industries came out in favour of the coal miners on 3 May 1926.

2.2 REASONS FOR THE GENERAL STRIKE'S FAILURE
Government readiness
By the time the Samuel Commission reported, the government was well prepared for a major industrial strike. The Organisation for the Maintenance of Supplies was created

to train volunteer strike breakers to drive trucks and assist with the distribution of fuel and food.

Baldwin's tactics
Baldwin cleverly organised the government's case by presenting the strike as a conflict between elected constitutional government and the trade unions. The government launched a newspaper, the *British Gazette*, to convey the message, and its control of BBC radio was also important. All this generated considerable public backing.

The TUC's unreadiness
Although the TUC supported the miners, it was not prepared to fight a long strike for fear of placing too great a strain on trade union funds. The miners continued to strike until the autumn, when they were forced back to work rather than face starvation. Their refusal to accept the Samuel Commission recommendations meant they had to accept the owners' terms for returning to work.

2.3 CONSEQUENCES OF THE GENERAL STRIKE
General consequences
The defeat of the General Strike brought an end to syndicalist beliefs that employers and the government could be forced into giving concessions by mass industrial action. The main advantage that accrued to workers was that it helped persuade employers against cutting wages in the late 1920s.

The Trades Disputes Act, 1927
This Act declared sympathetic strikes to be illegal and altered the rules governing the political levy. In future, if trade unionists wished to pay the levies, they had to 'opt in' rather than 'opt out', a change which reduced contributions to the Labour Party.

GLOSSARY

staple industry: a major industry in terms of size and level of employment.
subsidise: to support out of public funds.
commission: an inquiry set up by the government to report back with recommendations for action.

EXAMINER'S TIP

This topic appears at AS in the Edexcel and OCR specifications. If you have to assess sources, use factual information to place the sources in historical context. At AS you might be asked to explain why the General Strike took place. It is important to explain reasons in order of importance and to find links between them.

3 How great was the problem of unemployment in Britain in the 1930s?

3.1 BACKGROUND
In the 1920s, the unemployment rate stayed around 10% of the workforce, but after the *Wall Street Crash* of 1929 it rose to in excess of 50% in parts of the north of England, Scotland and Wales. A defining image of the 1930s is the Jarrow Crusade in 1936 when

hundreds of unemployed shipworkers marched to London to present a petition to the government.

3.2 THE EXTENT OF THE PROBLEM

Hard-hit northerners

Following the Wall Street Crash, the volume of international trade reduced to the detriment of British exports such as shipbuilding, coal and textiles. These staple industries were located in the northeast, Lancashire, Yorkshire, South Wales, Glasgow and Belfast. Unemployment levels in West Cumbria were in excess of 50%.

Soft southerners

In the south and Midlands the economy was very different. New electrical and car manufacturing industries thrived and this part of the economy was also aided by a housing boom and a buoyant construction industry. As a result, car-manufacturing towns like Luton and Dagenham experienced unemployment levels as low as 4%.

3.3 THE SOCIAL AND ECONOMIC IMPACT OF UNEMPLOYMENT

Assistance

Following the 1931 cuts in public expenditure, the government set up Public Assistance Committees to aid the unemployed via dole payments. Receipt of the dole was subject to a means test and payments could be reduced if a family member found employment. There were significant local variations in how the means test operated, and in 1934 the government established the Unemployment Assistance Board to ensure a universal application of relief payments.

The myth of the feckless poor re-emerged with opponents of government assistance pointing to an increase in and limited changes to alcohol and tobacco consumption.

The National Unemployed Workers' Movement

The NUWM dealt exclusively with problems of the unemployed and organised marches and demonstrations to pressurise the government towards making changes. (The Jarrow Crusade was not part of the NUWM.)

Political extremism

Oswald Mosley's British Union of Fascists gained considerable publicity and communism made some headway, with pockets of local communist support in places such as the South Wales coal field.

EXAMINER'S TIP

This topic appears at AS in the Edexcel and OCR specifications, at AS in AQA Alternative U (Britain 1929–1997) and at A2 in AQA Alternative Q (Britain 1895–1951). Learn, understand and use historical terms associated with this topic, such as 'staple industry', 'means test' and 'dole'. At AS you might be asked to explain how widespread the problem of unemployment was in the 1930s.

What did the national government do to try to end the Depression?

4.1 FINANCIAL POLICIES

Coming off the Gold Standard

When the *Gold Standard* was abandoned in 1931, the value of the pound stabilised around US$3.40. This stimulated business investment through a reduction in interest rates and aided the growth of suburban Britain because mortgage rates were linked to business rates.

Tariffs

In 1932, the government imposed a 10% tariff on imported goods, with the exceptions of those from the British empire. The tariffs helped protect industries such as iron and steel from foreign competition.

4.2 FURTHER MARKET INTERVENTION

Marketing boards

After 1933, marketing boards were created as part of the Ottawa Agreements on Empire Trade to assist in the distribution of foodstuffs such as milk and potatoes.

The Special Areas Act, 1934

This Act directed government assistance to areas of high unemployment such as West Cumbria and South Wales, and it was the first attempt at regional planning.

Rearmament

From 1937, the rise of Hitler and Mussolini prompted the British government to rearm. The pace of rearmament mounted following the Munich Crisis of September 1938 and led to increases in public expenditure, which, in turn, led to increases in demand. For example, the demand for naval ships aided areas such as the northeast.

Gold Standard: a method of organising trade whereby a national surplus or deficit in international trading resulted in either receiving or giving the balance in gold.

This topic appears at AS in the OCR and Edexcel specifications. It appears at AS in AQA Alternative U (Britain 1929–1997) and at A2 in AQA Alternative R (Britain 1895–1951). Learn, understand and use the historical terms associated with this topic, such as 'Gold Standard', 'special areas' and 'rearmament'. If you have to assess sources, use factual knowledge to place the sources in historical context. Try to use statistical data to support your arguments. At AS you might be expected to answer questions about what actions the national government took to deal with unemployment. At A2 you will be expected to produce a more balanced, analytical view which will require you to assess the degree of success of national government policy.

1   What was Britain's global position in 1918?

1.1 BACKGROUND

In 1918, Britain was one of the victorious Allies in the First World War. Although Britain remained one of the world's leading industrial and commercial nations, the USA had emerged as the global economic powerhouse.

1.2 THE BRITISH EMPIRE

Britain possessed the largest empire in the world, covering 25% of the Earth's surface and containing a third of the global population. Britain deployed the world's largest navy to defend empire interests which were divided into three types of administrative unit.

India

India was the most important and populous part of the empire and comprised the modern-day states of India, Pakistan, Bangladesh, Sri Lanka and Myanmar. The British Indian empire was controlled by a viceroy appointed by the British government and administered by a British secretary of state in the Cabinet and the India Office. An independence movement had developed under the leadership of the Indian National Congress.

The dominions

The empire also contained areas which had internal self-government with their own government and Parliament. These dominions were Australia, Canada, New Zealand, Newfoundland and South Africa.

The colonies

The rest of the empire comprised colonies controlled by a governor, who was appointed by the Colonial Office in London. Gibraltar, Jamaica and Hong Kong were examples of colonies.

EXAMINER'S TIP

This topic appears at A2 at Edexcel and AQA. Learn, understand and use historical terms associated with this subject, such as 'dominion'. You will be expected to use information from this section to provide a balanced, analytical answer.

2 How successful was Britain at the Paris Peace Conference, 1919–20?

2.1 BRITAIN, EUROPE AND THE USA

In European affairs Britain had traditionally supported a balance of power and it had entered the First World War to prevent German domination of Europe. In the period after 1918 Britain was the major European power, along with France. Germany was greatly weakened; Russia had turned communist and was isolated politically from the rest of Europe; the Austro-Hungarian empire had collapsed, to be replaced by several small states including Austria, Hungary and Czechoslovakia; the Ottoman empire had also collapsed and lost its non-Turkish territories in the Middle East.

The USA, having greatly aided the British and French against Germany, emerged from the First World War as the world's richest nation. However, it played a relatively small part in international affairs, and in the 1920s and 1930s entered a period of international isolation. The scene was set in 1919, when the US Congress defied President Wilson and refused to join the League of Nations or ratify the Treaty of Versailles.

2.2 LLOYD GEORGE, WILSON AND CLEMENCEAU

The British prime minister, Lloyd George, joined President Wilson of the US and Prime Minister Clemenceau of France in a triumvirate of world leaders who made the major decisions at the Paris Peace Conference.

In the December 1918 general election, Lloyd George had announced plans to build 'homes fit for heroes' and to provide pensions for the wounded, and for widows and orphans. This would cost a considerable amount of money and one of his ministers, Geddes, announced that he wanted to squeeze the Germans for money 'until the pips squeaked'.

In foreign policy, Lloyd George also wanted to prevent the outbreak of future war, to protect Britain's naval position and to stop the spread of communism in Europe. The communists had seized control of Russia in 1917 and there were communist attempts to seize power in Germany and Hungary in 1919. In these views Lloyd George occupied a position midway between those of Wilson and Clemenceau. Wilson wanted a just and fair peace, while Clemenceau wanted to destroy Germany's ability to wage war ever again.

2.3 THE TREATY OF VERSAILLES, 1919

The Treaty of Versailles set up the League of Nations as an international organisation to guarantee peace through collective security rather than the old system of maintaining a balance of power.

The Treaty of Versailles and Germany

Under the treaty, the Germans were forced to:
- admit they had caused the war
- pay reparations to the Allies, including Britain, to the sum (which was calculated by April 1921) of £6.6 billion
- lose territory in Europe to France, Belgium, Denmark and Poland
- lose their ocean-going fleet and have their army drastically reduced

- demilitarise the Rhineland area of western Germany and have it occupied by Allied troops

2.4 BRITISH GAINS

Two treaties followed the Paris Peace Conference and both altered Britain's position in the world.

The Treaty of Versailles, 1919

Germany lost its overseas territories which were administered by the British as League of Nations *mandates*: Britain controlled Tanganyika; South Africa controlled South West Africa; and Australia controlled North-East New Guinea.

The Treaty of Sèvres, 1920

Britain signed this treaty with Turkey and took over administration of the Middle East mandates of Palestine, Iraq and Transjordan.

3 What were the main problems facing Britain in foreign policy, 1920–33?

3.1 RELATIONS WITH GERMANY

War reparations

At the beginning of the 1920s, Britain's main aim was to receive *reparations* payments. However, between 1922 and 1924 Germany entered a period of major economic crisis associated with hyperinflation.

The Ruhr

In January 1923, a Franco-Belgian military force entered the Ruhr industrial area of Germany following a delay in the payment of reparations. They aimed to acquire goods and raw materials, but the occupation deepened the economic crisis and caused a political crisis in western Europe.

Compromise

The Labour government, under Ramsay MacDonald, helped negotiate the withdrawal of troops from the Ruhr. MacDonald also chaired a conference in London which accepted the American Dawes Plan. This helped Germany pay reparations with US loans.

The Locarno Treaty, 1925

In 1925, the British foreign secretary, Austen Chamberlain, signed the Locarno Treaty with France, Germany, Italy and Belgium. Germany recognised its new western borders (though not its borders in the east). In return, British and French occupation troops in the Rhineland were reduced and Germany was allowed to join the League of Nations.

Abandonment of German reparations

In 1929, Britain agreed to the US Young Plan to reorganise the German timetable for the payment of reparations. In 1932, reparations payments were suspended because of the economic depression.

3.2 DISARMAMENT AND WORLD PEACE

Negotiators at the Paris Peace Conference had major hopes of creating a more stable world and — although attempts at disarmament came to nothing — international peace-making efforts continued.

The Geneva Protocol, 1924

In 1924, Ramsay MacDonald attempted to increase the powers of the League of Nations through the Geneva Protocol. The aim was for League of Nations members to support world peace.

The Kellogg–Briand Pact, 1928

In 1928, Britain signed the Kellogg–Briand Pact and joined other signatory nations in denouncing the use of war as an instrument of policy.

3.3 RELATIONS WITH TURKEY

Following the Treaty of Sèvres with Turkey, a revolution in Turkey overthrew the Sultan and created a new Turkish Republic. This led to war between Greece and Turkey between 1920 and 1923.

Under the Treaty of Sèvres, Britain was pledged to defend the Dardanelles and Bosphorus Straits, which were placed under international control. In 1922, Turkey invaded the international zone in order to return the land to Turkey. The prime minister, Lloyd George, wanted to prevent this Turkish action — which was known as the Chanak crisis — but backed down because he did not receive support from the British empire dominions.

3.4 RELATIONS WITH COMMUNIST RUSSIA

Britain feared the Russian government's support of the idea of world communist revolution and accused Russia of trying to overthrow non-communist governments. In 1924, the Labour government recognised the Russian government but in 1927, following a police raid on the Russian trade delegation in London, diplomatic relations were severed.

3.5 RELATIONS WITH JAPAN

In 1922, Britain signed the Washington Naval Treaty with the USA and Japan to attempt naval disarmament in the Pacific.

In 1931, Japan occupied Manchuria in north China. Britain, with other members of the League of Nations, condemned the invasion and a Commission of Inquiry of the League was created under Lord Lytton. Lytton's report in 1932 reaffirmed the condemnation but also called on China to respect Japanese rights in China. It had no real effect, other than to cause Japan's resignation from the League of Nations in 1933.

reparations: the £6 billion worth of payments that Germany had to make to the Allies, having been forced by the Treaty of Versailles to admit that it had caused the First World War.

This topic appears at A2 in the AQA and Edexcel specifications. You will be asked to answer analytical questions such as 'How successful was Britain's foreign policy, 1920–33?' You should explain the aims of Britain's foreign policy as part of your assessment of the degree of success.

4 How did the British empire develop, 1918–39?

4.1 THE DOMINIONS

The Irish Free State and Southern Rhodesia (Zimbabwe) joined Australia, Canada, New Zealand, Newfoundland and South Africa as dominions of the British empire. The dominions gained considerable political independence and — at the 1926 Imperial Conference — the Balfour Declaration stated that they were independent states with the British monarch as head of state. This created the British Commonwealth.

These changes were included in the Statute of Westminster and from 1931 the dominions had full internal self-government and control over their foreign policies. In 1939, Canada declared war on Germany the day after Britain, but Eire (formally the Irish Free State) decided to stay neutral.

4.2 INDIA

The Indian National Congress

British rule faced a challenge from the Indian National Congress which, under the leadership of Ghandi and Nehru, engaged in campaigns of civil disobedience in 1919–22 and 1929–31. British reactions varied from the brutal to the legislative, and in 1919, General Dyer massacred a large number of demonstrators in Amritsar in the Punjab.

Government of India Act, 1919

After the Amritsar massacre, Britain introduced the Montagu–Chelmsford reforms under the Government of India Act. This created 11 self-governing provinces of British India with Indian ministers given control over public health, education and agriculture. The British viceroy retained control over finance, public order and foreign relations.

The Simon Commission

In 1927, the Conservative government set up the Simon Commission to report on the Montagu–Chelmsford reforms. In 1929, the commission suggested giving India dominion status and this was followed by Round Table Conferences in London between Britain and Indian representatives.

Government of India Act, 1935

In 1935, the Government of India Act handed control of the provinces to Indians. However, the viceroy still controlled India's central government.

4.3 THE MIDDLE EAST

Palestine

Britain faced major problems with the Palestine mandate. Within a mixed population of Jews and Arabs there, as much hostility, particularly over the question of Jewish immigration. In 1930, a White Paper outlined plans to restrict immigration, but it increased with the rise of Hitler and German anti-Semitism. An Arab revolt in 1936 led to the Peel Report of 1937 which recommended dividing Palestine into separate Jewish and Arab areas.

Egypt

In 1922, Britain gave independence to Egypt, but kept a military presence in the country.

5 Why did Britain adopt a policy of appeasement towards Germany and Italy?

5.1 BACKGROUND

During the 1930s, Mussolini's Italy and Hitler's Germany adopted aggressive foreign policies. Mussolini invaded and occupied Abyssinia (Ethiopia) in 1935–36 and Hitler unilaterally revised the Treaty of Versailles. Britain did not confront either state militarily. Instead it adopted a policy of *appeasement*.

5.2 REASONS FOR APPEASEMENT

Threats to the empire

Britain ran a world empire and in the 1930s faced potential threats from Japan, Italy and Germany. Britain did not have the military power to confront all three states at the same time.

Anti-war sentiment

Attitudes in Britain were against war, as shown by such events as the Peace Ballot referendum of 1935, which voted against war, and the victory of a pacifist candidate in the 1933 East Fulham by-election. Most British people feared another major war would be more destructive than the First World War and that peace should therefore be maintained, almost at all costs.

Economic depression

In the 1930s Britain faced an economic depression. Consequently, the government cut public expenditure and Britain didn't have the money to produce modern, well-equipped armed forces to confront Hitler and Mussolini.

5.3 THE FORMS OF APPEASEMENT BETWEEN 1933 AND 1938

Ignoring Churchill

From his position on the backbenches, Winston Churchill tried to raise the issue of secret German rearmament after 1933. His views were ignored.

The Stresa Front

In 1935, Britain joined the Stresa Front with France and Italy in an attempt to adopt a common approach to Germany's attitude to the Treaty of Versailles. It was formed in response to the German decision to reintroduce compulsory military service (conscription), but the front collapsed when Italy invaded Abyssinia.

The Italians in Abyssinia

British and French foreign ministers tried to appease Mussolini after the Italian invasion of Abyssinia in 1935. The Hoare–Laval Pact offered Mussolini two thirds of Abyssinia if he stopped the war. British public opinion and the House of Commons were outraged, Hoare was forced to resign and the pact collapsed.

The Anglo–German Naval Agreement

In 1935, Britain signed the Anglo–German Naval Agreement which broke the Treaty of Versailles. Britain agreed that Germany could increase the size of its navy.

The Germans in the Rhineland and Austria

In 1936, Hitler remilitarised the Rhineland in a clear breach of both the Treaty of Versailles and the Locarno Treaty. Britain and France took no action. In March 1938, Hitler forcibly united Austria with Germany in the Anschluss. Once again, Britain and France did nothing.

GLOSSARY

appeasement: a policy of agreeing to the demands of a hostile nation in the hope of maintaining peace.

EXAMINER'S TIP

This topic appears at A2 in the Edexcel, AQA and OCR (Germany only) specifications. Use the information to support and sustain analytical argument. If you have to assess sources, use the information in this section to place sources in historical context. You might be expected to produce an answer which compares one reason for the adoption of appeasement against others, such as 'How far were economic factors the reason why appeasement was adopted in the 1930s?'

6 | Was the Munich Agreement of September 1938 a success for Neville Chamberlain?

6.1 BACKGROUND

The Munich Agreement was signed between Britain, France, Germany and Italy, and handed the Sudetenland region of Czechoslovakia to Germany. There were 3.5 million Germans in the Sudetenland. Britain also signed a separate agreement with Germany, with both countries declaring they would never go to war with each other. On his return to London, Chamberlain famously declared: 'Peace in our time.'

The Munich Agreement is regarded as the best example of appeasement and Chamberlain was vilified for having signed it. He was regarded as a weak, naïve man who had been duped by Hitler, and appeasement was seen as a contributory cause of the Second World War.

6.2 CHAMBERLAIN'S MOTIVES

Chamberlain's personal view

Chamberlain disliked war, having experienced the trenches during the First World War. He wished fervently to avoid a repeated bloody conflict, particularly over German occupation of the Sudetenland.

An acceptance of German self-determination

Chamberlain, like many other British politicians, believed the Treaty of Versailles had been too harsh on Germany. This argument said that Versailles had based peace on the principle of national self-determination and that all Hitler requested in 1938 was to unite German-speaking peoples in one state.

Britain's unreadiness for war

Britain was not in a position to go to war with Germany over the Sudetenland in September 1938. The armed forces lacked equipment and numbers. The Royal Air Force, for example, was equipped mainly with bi-planes. In addition, German propaganda had given British politicians the impression that the German armed forces were larger than they really were.

Following the Munich Agreement, Chamberlain accelerated Britain's rearmament programme, suggesting he wasn't fooled by Hitler.

Fear of bombing

Chamberlain was advised by the Air Ministry that a major Anglo-German war would result in massive civilian casualties from aerial bombing. The Air Ministry estimated that 2 million casualties were likely if the war lasted 2 years, and the commonly held view was that 'the bomber will always get through'. A war, therefore, should be avoided at all costs.

Lack of Commonwealth support

In 1938, Britain did not have the support of the Commonwealth to go to war with Germany. Hertzog, the South African prime minister, said that his country would stay neutral if a war occurred over the Sudetenland. If Chamberlain had confronted Hitler militarily, he would almost certainly have split the British empire.

6.3 ALTERNATIVES TO APPEASEMENT

Military alliance

An alternative to appeasement and war in 1938 might have been a French–British–Russian alliance against Germany. However, many politicians in Britain disliked and feared Soviet Russia more than they feared Nazi Germany. In addition, military alliances had been blamed for causing the First World War.

Collective security

Another alternative to war might have been the *collective security* of the League of Nations. However, by 1938, the League had been discredited by Japan's invasion of Manchuria and Italy's invasion of Abyssinia. In addition, Germany, Japan, Italy and the USA were not League of Nations members in 1938.

GLOSSARY

collective security: an alternative idea to the balance of power for maintaining world peace, whereby all the members of the League of Nations would work together to support peace. As the League had no military power to back up its views, it proved ineffective.

EXAMINER'S TIP

This topic appears at A2 in the AQA, Edexcel and OCR specifications. Use the information in this section to support and sustain analytical argument. If you have to assess sources, remember to use factual information to place the sources in historical context. As this topic is open to different historical interpretations, it would be useful to include these in your answers.

7 Why did Britain go to war with Germany in September 1939?

7.1 INVASION OF CZECHOSLOVAKIA, 1939

At the Munich Agreement in September 1938, Hitler declared he had no more territorial claims in Europe. The following March, Germany broke the promise when its troops occupied the Czech-speaking areas of Bohemia and Moravia.

This proved that Hitler wanted to acquire territory which was not German-speaking and Britain realised that other eastern European states were now under German threat. As a result, in March 1939, Britain and France decided to guarantee Polish security.

7.2 SUPPORT FROM THE DOMINIONS

By the summer of 1939, the dominions had come to see that Hitler was a major threat to European peace. Therefore, they decided to fall in with Britain if (and when) it went to war with Germany.

7.3 REARMAMENT

By the late summer of 1939, Britain's war preparations included plans for the mass evacuation of children from cities, air defences, and naval and airforce rearmament. Conscription was introduced in April 1939, the first time compulsory military service had been required during peacetime.

7.4 THE NAZI–SOVIET PACT, 1939

Britain and France failed to form a defensive alliance with Soviet Russia. Instead, in August 1939, Russia signed a non-aggression pact with Hitler.

EXAMINER'S TIP

This topic appears at A2 in AQA Alternative R (Britain 1895–1951) and the Edexcel and OCR specifications. It appears at AS in AQA Alternative U (Britain 1929–1997). At AS you might be expected to explain why Britain went to war in 1939. At A2 you might be expected to explain why Britain went to war in September 1939 instead of September 1938. In this question you will have to use information from the last two sections.

UNIT 15 Britain in the Second World War, 1939–45

KEY QUESTIONS

(1) How did Britain's war aims change?

(2) What were the main areas of operation of British forces?

(3) What impact did the war have on the British economy and society?

1 How did Britain's war aims change?

1.1 PROTECTING POLAND: THE PHONEY WAR

Britain declared war to protect Poland. However, it had no military strategy for Poland's defence. Meanwhile, the Soviet invasion of east Poland and the Soviet Winter War with Finland created further military and foreign policy problems. Britain condemned Russian action but did nothing else.

From September 1939 to April 1940, in a period known as the phoney war, Britain did very little to attack Germany. In April 1940, Britain and France planned to occupy Norway to deny German access to Norwegian iron ore and naval bases. The Germans attacked first and occupied Norway and Denmark. Britain had also declared war to stop German aggression. Following the fall of Poland, Britain intervened in an attempt to stop the Germans taking Greece in 1941. This too was a failure.

1.2 OPPOSING ITALY, THEN JAPAN

Italy

Britain's war aims changed with the entry of Italy into the war from June 1940. Britain wanted to protect Egypt and the Suez Canal and to maintain naval supremacy in the Mediterranean.

From the fall of France in June 1940 until June 1941, Britain was involved in a struggle for survival as it fought Germany and Italy alone. In this period, Britain gained military aid and political support from the USA.

Japan

The Japanese invasion and occupation of Hong Kong, Malaya and Burma meant Britain had to defend its Asian empire and, in particular, India. In the Far East, Britain's main aim was the defeat of Japan and the recovery of its occupied imperial territories.

1.3 THE GRAND ALLIANCE

In June 1941, Germany invaded the USSR. Britain became an ally of the USSR and the following December Germany declared war against the USA. A Grand Alliance opposed to Nazi Germany was formed between the USA, the USSR and the British empire. Between the end of 1941 and 1945, the Grand Alliance met on several occasions and developed its war aims at:

- Casablanca, Morocco, in 1943 when Britain and the USA declared that they wanted the unconditional surrender of Germany
- Quebec, Canada, in August 1943 when Britain and the USA began planning the D-Day landings in Normandy
- Tehran, Iran, in 1943 when Britain, the USA and the USSR discussed the European theatre of war and the USSR's possible entry into the war against Japan

1.4 Yalta, February 1945

The most important Grand Alliance wartime meeting was in February 1945 at Yalta in the USSR. The USA, the USSR and Britain met to discuss the postwar settlement of Europe. Elections in Poland proved to be a major issue, as did the military division of Germany after the war, and the beginning of the collapse of the Grand Alliance was apparent at the Conference.

1.5 A moral imperative

Following the discovery of the concentration camps towards the end of the war, Britain's war aims changed slightly to include the need to defeat Germany on moral and human rights grounds. Nazi atrocities forced the Grand Alliance powers to set up the War Crimes trials to hold the Nazi leaders to account.

EXAMINER'S TIP

This topic appears at AS in AQA Alternative U (Britain 1929–1997) and in the OCR specification. Use the information in this section to explain how Britain's war aims changed during the course of the war.

2 What were the main areas of operation of British forces?

2.1 The Atlantic

In the Battle of the Atlantic, 1939–45, the German aim was to starve Britain into surrender. The Royal Navy fought German submarine, air and surface forces, which were attacking the merchant ships carrying vital war and food supplies from North America. The turning point came in 1943 when Britain developed more sophisticated detection equipment of U-boats, and captured the German secret code machine Enigma. The deployment of aircraft carriers on Atlantic convoy duty also helped swing the battle.

2.2 France

The British army was in France between September 1939 and June 1940. Following the fall of France and the Dunkirk evacuation, the troops retreated across the Channel and prepared for a German invasion.

2.3 The Middle East

The British army was in the Middle East to protect Egypt and the Suez Canal. Between 1940 and 1943, British and Commonwealth troops fought Italian and German forces in the Western Desert. Occupation of Libya and Tunisia laid the foundations for the invasion of Italy.

2.4 The Battle of Britain

Between June and September 1940, the RAF defended Britain during the Battle of Britain. After that, under the leadership of Sir Arthur Harris, RAF Bomber Command attempted to force Germany to surrender with massive aerial bombing of industrial and civilian targets. The RAF also assisted the navy in the Battle of the Atlantic.

2.5 Italy, D-Day and the Far East

From 1943 to 1945, British and US troops were engaged in the invasion and occupation of Italy. From June 1944 to April 1945, British, Canadian and US troops invaded and occupied north-western Europe following the D-Day invasions. In the Far East, British and Commonwealth forces were engaged in preventing the Japanese invasion of India and the recapture of occupied imperial territory.

EXAMINER'S TIP

This topic appears at AS in both the AQA and OCR specifications. Use the information in this section for general knowledge about Britain's participation in the Second World War.

3 What impact did the war have on the British economy and society?

3.1 POLITICAL LEADERSHIP

Declaration of war saw Neville Chamberlain continue as prime minister until he was forced to resign after the German occupation of Norway and Denmark in April 1940. Winston Churchill became prime minister on 10 May 1940 and led a coalition government which included Clement Attlee, the Labour leader, as deputy prime minister. Churchill remained leader throughout the war with little opposition other than a threatened vote of no confidence following the loss of Singapore in February 1942. Labour's main contribution to the war effort was in organising the Home Front, and Ernest Bevin played a key role.

3.2 THE IMPACT ON SOCIETY

Air raid precautions

At the outbreak of war there was a mass evacuation of children from cities to the countryside. Within areas likely to be bombed, air raid shelters were built. Large public shelters with the facility to house hundreds of people were built in public places. In London, underground stations were used. In private houses, Anderson shelters were built in gardens. Inside, a steel cage, known as a Morrison shelter, protected beds against falling debris if a house was bombed. The German bombers began their raids from the summer of 1940 in a campaign that lasted until 1942. From June 1944, London was attacked by V1 flying bombs and V2 rockets. Over 35,000 civilians died in air raids.

Rationing

From the beginning of the war, the Ministry of Supply determined a food allowance limited to 3,000 calories a day. Free milk and dinners were supplied to school children, and nurseries were set up for the children of women engaged in war work.

Food shortages intensified after German successes in decimating convoys during the Battle of the Atlantic, and a black market operated for extra or banned goods such as silk stockings. To supplement the food supply, everyone was encouraged to 'dig for victory' and all over Britain any open space that could be used for growing food was turned into an allotment.

The Emergency Powers Act, 1940

The Emergency Powers Act gave the government unprecedented scope to intervene in the lives of ordinary citizens and mobilise the economy. Jobs deemed vital to the war effort (e.g. coal mining) were classified as reserve occupations, and men employed in these industries were exempt from military conscription. In 1944, a shortage of coal meant that the so-called Bevin boys were conscripted to go down the mines rather than join the armed forces.

Women

In December 1941, the shortage of labour was such that the government introduced conscription of women under the National Service No. 2 Act. It applied to unmarried women, who were given the option of joining the armed forces in non-combat roles or the Land Army to work in agriculture, or of working in munitions factories. Between 1939 and 1943, the number of women employed rose by 50% to 2.2 million.

Propaganda

Morale-boosting included patriotic BBC broadcasts and cheerful programmes like the music-based *Workers' Playtime* and comedy shows such as Tommy Handley's *It's That Man Again*. Under Regulation 2D, newspapers engaged in self-censorship. Civilian letters were censored to prevent war information been transmitted and — under the slogan 'careless talk costs lives' — civilians were encouraged not to discuss the war.

3.3 SOCIAL CHANGES DURING THE WAR

Policy changes

The family means test was abolished in 1941 and in December 1942 a Report on Social Insurance and Allied Services (The Beveridge Report) recommended the creation of a welfare state after the war. Although Churchill and the Conservatives were frightened by the financial implications of the Beveridge Report (and attempted to scale it down), they were aware of its popularity.

The Education Act, 1944

This reorganised secondary education by creating three types of school: grammar schools; technical schools; and secondary modern schools. Allocation of pupils to schools was made through the 11-plus exam and the school leaving age was raised to 15 years.

3.4 FINANCE AND THE ECONOMY

The government introduced central planning and the Ministries of Supply and Production organised the war industries. Coal mines and railways came under government direction.

By 1945, 83% of Britain's public expenditure was on military and defence requirements with the country also having to pay for war damage caused by aerial bombing and the loss of a significant part of the merchant navy. Britain had built up a £13 billion debt.

From the spring of 1941, Britain received *lend-lease* from the USA which amounted to a form of wartime loan due to be paid back once the war was over.

EXAMINER'S TIP

This topic appears at AS in the AQA specification. Use the information in this section to explain the extent to which British society and the economy were affected by the Second World War.

KEY QUESTIONS

(1) Why did the Labour Party win the 1945 general election?

(2) How successful were Labour's social, economic and welfare reforms, 1945–51?

(3) How successful was Labour's foreign policy, 1945–51?

(4) How effective was Labour's handling of imperial issues, 1945–51?

(5) How successful were the Labour governments, 1964–70 and 1974–79?

(6) Why did the Labour Party decline and recover, 1979–97?

1 Why did the Labour Party win the 1945 general election?

1.1 THE ELECTORAL SYSTEM

As a result of population movements, urban constituencies had an average of 6,000 fewer voters than rural and suburban constituencies. Labour traditionally received support from urban areas and the *single majority system of voting* exaggerated the scale of Labour victory. In 1945, Labour won 383 seats with 47.8% of the vote while the Conservatives won 213 seats with 39.8% of the vote.

1.2 DESIRE FOR A CHANGE

The Conservatives had dominated the 1931–45 national governments and many people wanted a change. There were strong memories of the Depression, and Labour support of the Beveridge Report and its plans for nationalisation of major industries proved an attraction to voters.

1.3 THE ELECTION CAMPAIGN

Labour blamed the Conservatives for appeasement in the late 1930s and accused them of helping to start the Second World War. The Labour leader, Clement Attlee, received credit for his part in the war effort. He had been deputy prime minister from 1940 and came across as a moderate statesman. The majority of servicemen voted Labour.

The Conservative election campaign was based mainly on Churchill's wartime leadership. Churchill was seen as a good war leader, but he was thought likely to be a poor leader in peacetime, and his warning that Labour would introduce a Gestapo-style police force backfired. Unlike Labour, the Conservatives lacked clear policies and produced their election manifesto in a few weeks. In addition, the Conservative Party organisation had declined during the war due, in part, to the military service of many party organisers.

GLOSSARY

single majority system of voting: based on the idea that a candidate with the most votes wins, even though he or she might not have an overall majority of votes cast. This creates a disparity between the percentage of votes received and the number of seats won.

EXAMINER'S TIP

This topic appears at AS in AQA Alternative U (Britain 1929–1997) and the OCR specification. It also appears at A2 in AQA Alternative R (Britain 1895–1951). Learn, understand and use historical terms associated with this topic, such as 'single majority system of voting' and 'The Beveridge Report'. At AS you might be expected to answer questions which require you to explain the Labour landslide victory of 1945. You should place and explain the reasons for Labour's victory in order of importance. You might also be able to find links between reasons. At A2 you will be expected to assess and analyse the different factors resulting in Labour victory. You might be asked to explain how far the impact of the war assisted Labour victory and to compare this with other reasons.

2 How successful were Labour's social, economic and welfare reforms, 1945–51?

2.1 BACKGROUND TO ECONOMIC REFORMS

Britain had experienced central government control over the economy during the Second World War. Labour planned to ensure government control over the economy in peacetime. They created a planned economy where the government would control key sectors of the economy, such as energy and transport.

2.2 KEYNESIANISM

Labour was greatly influenced by the economic ideas of the Liberal economist John Maynard Keynes. Keynes believed governments could control the level of inflation and unemployment through increasing or decreasing public expenditure or taxation. Keynesian demand management economics was the dominant economic view in Britain from the end of the Second World War to 1976.

2.3 NATIONALISATION

Nationalisation involved 20% of British industry. The extension of government control over the economy included bringing the following into public ownership:

- the Bank of England, 1946
- civil aviation, 1946
- coal, 1947
- telecommunications, 1947
- railways, road haulage, road passenger transport and canals, 1948
- electricity, 1948
- gas, 1949
- iron and steel, 1950

The nationalisation of coal and the railways saved these industries from almost certain collapse. However, nationalised industries had a chequered history of economic efficiency. Nevertheless, the Labour Party laid the foundations of postwar economic prosperity where full employment was maintained alongside low inflation. Although rationing continued into the early 1950s, the standard of living had risen by 1951.

The iron and steel industry was denationalised by the Conservatives in the early 1950s and renationalised by Labour in the 1960s. Most of the industries listed above were privatised during the Thatcher and Major Conservative governments.

2.4 OTHER FACTORS IN ECONOMIC GROWTH

Economic growth was also aided by:

- the US Marshall Aid, which amounted to £1.26 billion between 1948 and 1952
- a devaluation of the pound in August 1949 from $4.03 to $2.8, which made imports dearer and exports cheaper
- wage restraint by trade unions, which kept business costs down

2.5 EDUCATION AND HEALTH

The Labour Party created the welfare state, a comprehensive plan to provide education and health care which was free at the point of use for all the population.

The 1944 Butler Education Act had laid the foundations for the postwar state education system.

Health was the main Labour reform and it fell to Aneurin Bevan to lead the formation of the National Health Service (NHS) in 1948. This provided free health care for all for the first time but quickly became overwhelmed by demand. The NHS budget rose from £128 million in 1948 to £228 million in 1949, and to £356 million in 1950. In 1949, the government introduced prescription charges of 5p (1 shilling) per item and in consequence Bevan and Harold Wilson resigned from the Cabinet.

2.6 OTHER REFORMS

Housing

This was also the responsibility of Aneurin Bevan and his aims were to rebuild homes destroyed by bombing and to reduce the number of slums. Prefabricated houses (prefabs) were the short-term solution, and by 1948, 150,000 had been produced.

The New Towns Act, 1946, laid down plans for new towns around large urban *conurbations,* and towns such as Crawley in Sussex and Stevenage in Hertfordshire were built. Other legislation ruled that houses were to be built with inside lavatories, and Bevan increased the size of council houses from 750 square feet to 900 square feet per family.

Unemployment benefit

Two Acts of Parliament laid the foundations of the modern social security system. The National Insurance Act, 1946, extended the 1911 Act to cover the whole population. The National Assistance Act, 1948, set up the National Assistance Board for those who needed extra financial help in addition to National Insurance payments. The means test was abolished.

Families

The government introduced family allowances, whereby parents received a weekly payment for each child born.

Pensions

In 1946, the single person's pension rose to £1.30 a week, the first rise since 1920.

conurbations: large urban areas comprising more than one town or city, e.g. the West Midlands.
nationalisation: bringing into public ownership. Nationalised industries were government controlled.

EXAMINER'S TIP

This topic appears at AS in AQA Alternative U (Britain 1929–1997) and the OCR specification. It appears at A2 in AQA Alternative Q (Britain 1895–1951). Learn, understand and use historical terms associated with this topic, such as 'nationalisation', 'welfare state' and 'demand management economics'. In AQA Alternative Q you will be expected to study the topic for the Unit 3 course essay. Use the information in this section as the basis of notes that you can use when you write the essay. At AS you may be expected to explain why these reforms were passed. You may also be asked to explain what changes the reforms brought about. At A2 you will be expected to produce balanced, analytical answers where factual knowledge is used to support and sustain argument. You might be asked to what extent the Labour reforms brought about a social and economic revolution in Britain. In this question you would have to define the word 'revolution' as part of your analysis.

3 | *How successful was Labour's foreign policy, 1945–51?*

3.1 BACKGROUND

The Cold War era began after 1945 with the world divided between the USSR and its allies and the USA and its allies. Britain — a world power in 1939 — had declined in importance, but Labour attempted to maintain its position.

3.2 POTSDAM, AUGUST 1945

Attlee attended the second Potsdam Conference following Labour's win in the July 1945 election. He agreed to the four-power military division of Austria and Germany, and pledged British responsibility for the military occupation and administration of parts of Austria and Germany, and their two capitals Vienna and Berlin. He also agreed to the forced repatriation of thousands of anti-communists to Yugoslavia and the USSR.

3.3 GREECE AND TURKEY

Britain aided anti-communist forces in the Greek Civil War and offered military assistance to Turkey. By 1947, Britain was not in an economic position to maintain its commitments. After Britain had formally announced its withdrawal, the USA took over Britain's role in these areas.

3.4 THE TRUMAN DOCTRINE

As the USSR established communist governments across eastern Europe, Britain supported the USA's tough stance against the spread of communism. The Truman Doctrine of March 1947 was supported by the Labour government. In return Britain benefited considerably from US economic aid.

3.5 THE BERLIN AIRLIFT

In 1948, Britain and the USA created Bizonia, a currency union within their two areas of German occupation. The USSR responded by blockading west Berlin, and the Berlin airlift was a joint US–British operation which flew in supplies until Stalin, the Soviet leader, ended the blockade in 1949.

3.6 NATO

The British foreign minister, Ernest Bevin, was a prime mover behind the creation of the North Atlantic Treaty Organisation (NATO) in 1949. This military alliance to defend western Europe from Russian attack was dominated by the USA and included Britain, Canada, France, the Benelux countries, Italy, Denmark, Norway and Iceland.

3.7 KOREA

In 1950, Britain supplied military forces to the United Nations contingent of troops which were defending South Korea in the Korean War, 1950–53. The resulting British rearmament damaged economic recovery.

This topic appears at AS in AQA Alternative U (Britain 1929–1997) and the OCR specification. It appears at A2 in AQA Alternative R (Britain 1895–1951). At AS you might be asked to explain how British foreign policy changed between 1945 and 1951. At A2 you will be expected to offer a balanced answer to questions such as 'How successfully did Britain adjust to its new position in foreign policy between 1945 and 1951?'

4 How effective was Labour's handling of imperial issues, 1945–51?

4.1 BACKGROUND

At the end of the Second World War, Britain still had a large overseas empire covering 25% of the world's land surface and containing a third of the world's population. However, Britain was virtually bankrupt, had major European military commitments and faced a rise of nationalism which led to the decline of empire and its replacement with the Commonwealth.

By 1945, parts of the British empire had already gained independence. These included Australia, Canada, New Zealand, South Africa, Newfoundland and Eire.

4.2 INDIAN PARTITION

'Quit India'

In 1945, the British Indian empire comprised the modern-day states of India, Pakistan, Sri Lanka, Myanmar and Bangladesh. The campaign for Indian independence had existed since the beginning of the century, and in the interwar period the Indian National Congress had organised civil disobedience campaigns to try to force Britain to leave India. In 1942, Ghandi, the Indian nationalist leader, organised the Quit India campaign and India was promised self-rule once the war came to an end.

Britain left India because it could no longer militarily control an area which had become a major financial burden.

Religious conflict

Indian nationalism was complicated by religious differences. Most of the population were Hindus, but a significant minority were Muslims. Most of these joined Mohammed Ali Jinnah's Muslim League and campaigned for a separate Muslim state.

Mountbatten

The appointment of Earl Mountbatten as the last viceroy of India in 1947 was a prelude to the rapid partition of India. He speeded up British withdrawal to a tight deadline and

UNIT 16

accepted the view that India should be partitioned between Hindu and Muslim states. On 15 August 1947, the independent states of India and Pakistan were created as dominions of the British Commonwealth. Pakistan was divided into two elements: West Pakistan (now Pakistan) and East Pakistan (now Bangladesh).

Post-1947

Major population movements occurred as Muslims and Hindus migrated to their respective states. A Muslim state, Kashmir, was occupied by India and sparked off a war with Pakistan in 1948–49. In 1948, Britain gave independence to Myanmar (then known as Burma) and Sri Lanka (then known as Ceylon). Ceylon joined the Commonwealth but Burma refused.

4.3 BRITISH WITHDRAWAL FROM PALESTINE

After the Second World War, Britain faced opposition from armed Jewish groups who wanted to create an independent state. In 1946, a terrorist bomb destroyed the King David Hotel, the British HQ in Palestine. Attempts to stop Jewish immigration failed and — mainly due to economic reasons — Britain was forced to withdraw from Palestine in 1947. It handed over control to the United Nations, and in 1948 the area was partitioned between the Jewish state of Israel and the Arab state of Jordan.

4.4 COLONIAL DEVELOPMENTS

In 1948, the government established the Colonial Development Corporation in an attempt to improve colonial economic development. Its major work was the East Africa Groundnut Scheme, an unpopular failure which came to an end in 1949.

EXAMINER'S TIP

This topic appears at AS in AQA Alternative U (Britain 1929–1997) and in the OCR specification. It is an A2 topic in AQA Alternative R (Britain 1895–1951). At AS you might be expected to explain why Britain adopted a policy of decolonisation. At A2 you might be expected to assess the degree of success of Labour policy towards the British empire. In answering this type of question, you would need to explain Labour's aims in imperial policy. Did Labour stick to its aims or were its actions dictated by circumstances?

5 How successful were the Labour governments, 1964–70 and 1974–79?

5.1 THE SIMILARITIES

Labour only had a working majority between 1966 and 1970. Otherwise there were marked similarities between its two periods in office, including:
- the need to work with a small majority or to form a *minority government*
- economic crises
- division into right- and left-wing factions
- trade union influence

5.2 LABOUR GOVERNMENT, 1964–70
Economic planning

The prime minister Harold Wilson attempted to extend government influence with the

Department for Economic Affairs under George Brown. Its aim was to direct investment into new technology, but it failed to deliver much due to the hostility of the Treasury and the 1967 economic crisis.

Devaluation

By November 1967, Britain was importing far more than it was exporting and there was a *balance of payments crisis*. To rectify the problem, the government devalued the pound. However, any beneficial economic effects were counterbalanced by the political humiliation that devaluation represented.

Industrial relations

British economic output was adversely affected by strikes. The government's Donovon Commission investigated industrial relations and produced the *In Place of Strife* White Paper of 1969. This aimed to outlaw *wildcat or unofficial strikes* and trade union opposition forced the government to back down.

Educational reforms

The education minister, Anthony Crosland, introduced comprehensive schools, and the Open University for distance, adult learning began.

Social reforms

The 1964–67 Labour government introduced many social reforms:
- abolition of the death penalty, 1965
- legalisation of homosexuality, 1967
- legalisation of abortion, 1967
- the Equal Pay Act, 1970, which established the principle of women receiving equal pay for equal work
- the Race Relations Acts, 1965 and 1968, which created the Race Relations Board and outlawed racism
- the Immigration Act, 1968, which restricted the right of entry to Britain of groups such as East African Asians
- the Representation of the People Act, 1969, which gave the vote to over-18s

Northern Ireland

Rioting over civil rights in 1968 and 1969 led the government to send troops to Northern Ireland in August 1969 to protect the Catholic community. It was the beginning of the Troubles, which lasted until 1998.

Rhodesia

Southern Rhodesia (Zimbabwe) declared independence from Britain, rather than see the end to white rule. Wilson failed to persuade the Rhodesian prime minister, Ian Smith, to back down in talks held on HMS *Tiger*.

Failure to join the EEC

Britain's application to join the European Economic Community in 1967 was vetoed by France under General de Gaulle.

5.3 REASONS WHY LABOUR LOST THE 1970 GENERAL ELECTION

Labour entered the campaign ahead in the opinion polls and Wilson was confident he could win the 1970 general election. However, Labour's election organisation was complacent and, shortly before the election, economic figures showing a rise in inflation led many voters to switch to the Conservatives.

5.4 LABOUR GOVERNMENT, 1974–79

Minority governments

Between the February and October elections of 1974, and between 1978 and 1979, Labour had to form minority governments. From the spring of 1977, Labour was kept in power only by Liberal Party support. This made the task of government a difficult one.

Economic planning

In 1974, the government founded the National Enterprise Board (NEB) to direct public money to key industries like computer technology. The NEB's impact diminished from 1976 and public money was used to save the troubled British Leyland car company. Planning proved difficult in the face of energy, labour and financial crises.

Energy crises

The Labour Party formed its 1974 government in the middle of a miners' strike and with the country working a 3-day week. The fourfold increase in oil prices from October 1973 had thrown the world economy into recession and inflation was increasing.

Labour crises

Labour ended the miners' strike by agreeing to a large increase in wages. Other public sector workers, such as teachers, received large pay increases and the totality of wage rises fuelled inflation. To try to limit pay demands, the government formed a voluntary pay restraint agreement under the Social Contract with the trade unions.

Referendum on EEC membership,1975

Britain had joined the European Economic Community (EEC) under the Conservatives in 1973, but the Labour Party was badly divided over the issue. Wilson defused internal party tensions with a national *referendum* on EEC membership. The yes vote to stay in was considerable.

Referenda on Scottish and Welsh devolution, 1979

The Devolution Act, 1978, granted self-government to Scotland and Wales, on condition that the electorates of both countries voted for the proposal. In both referenda devolution was rejected.

Northern Ireland

The Ulster Loyalist Workers' Strike destroyed the Power Sharing Executive created by the Sunningdale Agreement. Labour's attempt to get the peace process moving with an elected convention failed. The Northern Ireland secretary ended internment, and the Diplock courts were introduced to try terrorist suspects.

North Sea oil

The first production of North Sea oil became available.

5.5 REASONS WHY LABOUR LOST THE 1979 GENERAL ELECTION

The financial crisis

An accumulation of crises led to a financial crisis. The value of the pound declined against other currencies and, to prevent financial collapse, Britain raised loans from the Shah of Iran and the International Monetary Fund (IMF). The IMF demanded a major change in British economic policy whereby Keynesian demand management was replaced by monetarism. This was based on the control of the money supply and controlling inflation via raised interest rates and cuts in public expenditure.

The Winter of Discontent

Cuts in public expenditure led to public sector strikes in the winter of 1978–79 — the Winter of Discontent. This was a major reason for the defeat of the Labour Party in the 1979 election.

balance of payments crisis: the balance of payments is the account monitoring a country's trade with the rest of the world. There is a crisis when imports are much greater than exports.

minority government: a government which does not have an overall majority in the House of Commons.

referendum: a vote on one specific issue.

wildcat or unofficial strike: a strike not supported by the leadership of a trade union, but which is usually organised locally by shop stewards, the elected union representatives for a factory or part of a factory.

This topic appears at AS in the OCR specification (up to 1964). It also appears at A2 in AQA Alternative U (Britain 1929–1997). At AS you might be expected to explain what changes were made by the Wilson government, 1964–70. At A2 you might have to compare the performances of Wilson's governments in the 1960s and 1970s.

6 | Why did the Labour Party decline and recover, 1979–97?

6.1 THE DECLINE, 1979–83

Party splits

There was a growing split between left and right in the party. James Callaghan — who had replaced Wilson as prime minister in 1976 — resigned after the 1979 election. Michael Foot took over as leader and Tony Benn challenged the right winger Denis Healey for the deputy leadership. Benn lost by a narrow margin, but other internal developments shifted the party to the left.

A comparison of Labour and Tory leaders

The weak leadership of Michael Foot failed to keep the Labour Party together. Meanwhile, the Conservative prime minister Margaret Thatcher appeared strong in forcing through the economic changes of 1979–83 and in the British victory over Argentina in the Falklands War, 1982.

The SDP

In 1981, four right-wing Labour MPs — David Owen, Roy Jenkins, Shirley Williams and Bill Rodgers — left the party to form the Social Democratic Party. The SDP rose rapidly in popularity and several other Labour MPs defected to join its ranks. It joined forces with the Liberals in the 1983 election to form the Liberal/SDP Alliance.

The 1983 general election

The 1983 Labour manifesto was unpopular in advocating more public ownership, an anti-nuclear defence policy and major social reforms. In the 1983 general election, Labour won 209 seats with 27.6% of the vote, its worst performance since the 1930s. The Liberal/SDP Alliance won 25.4% of the vote, almost forcing Labour into third place in the electoral vote.

6.2 THE RECOVERY, 1983–92

Kinnock and the 1987 election

Neil Kinnock became Labour leader in 1984 and began a reorganisation of the party and its policies. At the 1985 Labour Conference he denounced the Militant Tendency faction which controlled Liverpool City Council. 'Militant', led by Derek Hatton, was in favour of large-scale public spending and maintaining high levels of public sector employment by the City Council. Kinnock abandoned Labour's anti-EEC and extreme socialist policies and appointed Peter Mandelson as director of communications in 1986. Mandelson relaunched Labour's image with a red rose and in the 1987 election, Labour's vote rose to 30.8% and it won 229 seats.

Conservative unpopularity and the 1992 election

The Conservatives' poll tax led to riots in London and the government also lost a series of by-elections, notably in the Tory heartland of Ribble Valley. The poll tax was subsequently abolished, but the Conservatives had other problems as economic recession deepened from 1989 to 1992 and unemployment rose. In the 1992 election, Labour almost won with 271 seats and 35% of the vote. Kinnock's failure in two elections led to his resignation and he was replaced by John Smith, who died prematurely in 1994.

6.3 ELECTORAL VICTORY, 1997

Labour — now rechristened New Labour and under the leadership of Tony Blair — won 419 seats compared to the Conservatives' 165. It was the biggest Conservative defeat since 1832 and happened for several reasons:

- Blair's continued reform of the Labour Party, including the removal of Clause 4 from the party constitution, thereby abandoning the party's commitment to public ownership
- the ability of New Labour to market itself as a moderate, modernising party
- the desire for change following nearly two decades of Conservative government
- the fiasco of leaving the European Exchange Rate Mechanism in 1992, which undermined confidence in the Conservative government's ability to run the economy
- the weakness of John Major's leadership of the Conservative government, which allowed a split to develop between pro- and anti-EU members
- political *sleaze* involving Conservative MPs such as Neil Hamilton

GLOSSARY

sleaze: political corruption which took the form of accepting cash for asking parliamentary questions, plus other attempts to influence Parliament.

EXAMINER'S TIP

This topic appears at A2 in AQA Alternative U (Britain 1929–1997). You will be expected to analyse the reasons for Labour's decline and subsequent recovery. This may involve balanced analysis where one reason is compared to others.

UNIT 17 — The Conservative Party, 1945–97

(1) What factors explain the Conservative recovery after the 1945 general election?

(2) How successful was Conservative domestic policy, 1951–64?

(3) How effectively did the Conservatives deal with foreign and imperial policy, 1951–64?

(4) How successful was Heath as prime minister, 1970–74?

(5) How successful was Thatcher as prime minister, 1979–90?

(6) How successful was Major as prime minister, 1990–97?

1 What factors explain the Conservative recovery after the 1945 general election?

1.1 PARTY REORGANISATION

Lord Woolton was appointed Conservative chairman in July 1946 and his party reorganisation involved:

- a membership drive, which by the early 1950s had recruited 3 million members
- the Woolton Fighting Fund, which restored the party's finances
- formation of the Young Conservatives in 1946 to encourage young people to join the party
- the Maxwell-Fyfe report of 1949, which resulted in a more democratic party organisation

1.2 POLICY CHANGES

'The Industrial Charter'

In 1947, the Conservatives published 'The Industrial Charter', a document which supported individual enterprise in society. While it abandoned the free market policies of the 1930s, it accepted cooperation in industry and recognised the role of trade unions.

The charter was the work of a policy-making body led by R. A. Butler, who was leader of the Advisory Committee on Policy and Political Education and who revived the Conservative Research Department as a think tank on policy development.

'The Right Road for Britain'

Determined not to repeat its ill-preparedness for the 1945 general election, the Conservatives published 'The Right Road for Britain' which acted as a manifesto for the 1950 general election.

1.3 IMPACT OF THE COLD WAR

Opposition to the USSR led to claims that the Cold War was a fight which pitted freedom and democracy against government control and dictatorship. Books like George Orwell's *1984*, published in 1948, emphasised the trend towards dictatorship in the parts of Europe under communist control.

1.4 THE 1950 AND 1951 GENERAL ELECTIONS

Labour narrowly won the 1950 general election with 315 seats to the Conservatives' 298, but Attlee's government had problems keeping control of its Commons majority.

A second general election, in October 1951, resulted in a narrow Conservative majority with 321 seats compared to Labour's 295. The Conservatives gained 48% of the vote compared to 48.8% for Labour.

EXAMINER'S TIP

This topic appears at AS in the OCR specification. Use the information to explain why the Conservatives won the 1951 general election and were returned to power.

2 How successful was Conservative domestic policy, 1951–64?

2.1 RISE IN THE STANDARD OF LIVING

The Conservatives were able to end rationing and benefited from the postwar economic boom which followed western Europe's recovery from the Second World War. Between 1951 and 1963 average wages rose by 72%. It was the beginning of the *affluent* society in Britain. New leisure pursuits such as television and pop music characterised the period, and the Conservative prime minister Harold Macmillan (1957–63) claimed: 'We never had it so good.'

2.2 ECONOMIC POLICY

The government followed Keynesian demand management economics using changes in taxation and public expenditure in an attempt to maintain low unemployment and taxation. However, this led to stop/go economic development, where economic growth fuelled inflation and was followed by an economic slowdown caused by tax rises to control inflation.

Stop/go economics discouraged investment in British industry and by 1964 Britain was in relative economic decline. West Germany and Japan had recovered economically and were challenging Britain's position as the West's second most important economy after the USA.

2.3 OTHER POLICIES

Housing

Conservatives made new house building a major priority. On average 330,000 houses a year were built in the mid-1950s. This brought an end to the housing shortage. However, building high-rise blocks of flats created social problems for the future.

Maintaining the welfare state

The Conservatives kept the main features of the welfare state, in particular the National Health Service. They even added to its provision under the Mental Health Act, 1959. The Conservatives raised prescription charges.

Education

The Conservatives maintained the provisions of the 1944 Education Act. However, support of grammar schools wavered in the early 1960s when some government members began to back the idea of comprehensive schools.

Higher education advanced with new universities planned in Warwick, York, Sussex and Essex and the opening of polytechnics offering scientific and engineering qualifications.

2.4 FAILURE TO JOIN THE EEC

In the 1950s, Britain avoided moves towards western European economic union. Britain did not join in the Schumann Plan for a European Coal and Steel Community and, in 1957, failed to sign the Treaty of Rome which created the European Economic Community (EEC). In 1961, the government finally decided to apply for EEC membership, but the application was turned down by France.

2.5 REASONS WHY THE CONSERVATIVES LOST THE 1964 GENERAL ELECTION

The Establishment factor

The Conservative government was criticised as being dominated by public school, Oxbridge-educated men. Macmillan, who was in his sixties, seemed tired and out of touch with society. Conservatives had been in power since 1951 and many of the electorate felt the government had run out of steam. This dissatisfaction was shown in the Orpington by-election, 1962, when a Conservative seat went to the Liberals with a 27% swing.

Foreign policy and immigration

The withdrawal from empire and the failure to join the EEC raised concerns about Britain's future position in the world. West Indian and Asian immigration also caused concern and the force of public opinion led to the restrictions imposed by the Commonwealth Immigration Act, 1962.

Reshuffles and scandals

In an attempt to show dynamic leadership, Macmillan changed 39 out of 101 ministerial posts in the Night of the Long Knives, July 1962. It was a miscalculation which lowered party morale. Confidence then plummeted with the Profumo sex scandal, 1962–63, a revelation that the minister of war had had an affair with a prostitute who was known to have had another affair with a Russian military attaché. Profumo lied about it to the House of Commons and his forced resignation further undermined the government's reputation.

Macmillan's resignation, 1963

Harold Macmillan resigned and was replaced by Lord Home, who emerged into the House of Commons as Sir Alec Douglas Home. The selection of an Establishment man like Home was criticised as an undemocratic choice made by a group of Old Etonians, and their man proved a feeble political campaigner without the skills needed to appear good on television.

Wilson's election as Labour leader, 1963

Hugh Gaitskell, Attlee's replacement as Labour leader in 1955, died in 1963. His death ended a period of Labour conflict between moderates led by Gaitskell and radicals associated with Aneurin Bevan. Harold Wilson reunited the party and gave it a modern, forward-looking image.

affluent: wealthy.

UNIT 17

EXAMINER'S TIP

This topic appears at AS in the OCR specification and A2 in AQA Alternative U (Britain 1929–97). At AS you might be expected to explain why the Conservatives held power for so long. If so, place and explain the reasons in order of importance. At A2 you might be expected to assess the importance of one reason against others in an explanation of Conservative dominance from 1951 to 1964. You might also be expected to explain why the Conservatives lost the 1964 general election.

3 How effectively did the Conservatives deal with foreign and imperial policy, 1951–64?

3.1 THE COLD WAR

The USSR

Britain played a big part in the defence of western Europe against the USSR. British armed forces occupied northern Germany and part of west Berlin. They also occupied part of Austria and part of Vienna. In 1955, the Austrian State Treaty saw the withdrawal of all foreign armed forces from Austria.

Nuclear weapons

In 1952, Britain exploded its own atom bomb and joined the USA and the USSR as a world nuclear power. During the 1950s, British nuclear bombs were carried by the RAF's V-bombers and, in the 1960s, the Royal Navy took over nuclear responsibility when Britain purchased Polaris nuclear submarines from the USA. Attempts to develop a separate British rocket technology failed with the cancellation of the Blue Streak rocket. In 1963, Britain signed the Test Ban Treaty with the USA and the USSR to ban nuclear tests in the atmosphere.

Cuba

Britain's position at the high table of diplomatic negotiation meant that during the 1962 Cuban missile crisis the British government was kept informed of developments by the USA.

Korea

In the Korean War, 1950–53, Britain supported the United Nations by deploying military forces.

3.2 WITHDRAWAL FROM EMPIRE

Independence

The Conservatives continued Labour's *decolonisation* policy and had to deal with numerous violent rebellions against British rule. By the time the Conservatives left office in 1964, the following countries had gained independence:

- Ghana, formerly the Gold Coast
- Malaya
- North Borneo and Sarawak
- Nigeria
- Kenya
- Uganda
- Tanganyika
- Zanzibar

Kenya and Malaya

The Mau Mau rebellion against British rule in Kenya in the early 1950s was suppressed, as was opposition from communist guerrillas in Malaya up to 1957.

Cyprus

In the late 1950s, Britain faced a Greek guerrilla attempt to unite Cyprus with Greece. The EOKA guerrilla force was not suppressed, but Cyprus became an independent state in the Commonwealth in 1960.

Rhodesia

In 1960, a Central African Federation was created out of Northern and Southern Rhodesia and Nyasaland. This collapsed in December 1963 and resulted in the independence of Northern Rhodesia as Zambia and of Nyasaland as Malawi.

South Africa

The granting of independence to black African nations caused friction with the white supremacist government of South Africa. The massacre of black demonstrators in Sharpeville in 1961 caused outrage across the Commonwealth, and South Africa left the Commonwealth to become a republic.

3.3 THE SUEZ CRISIS, 1956

The Suez Crisis led to the resignation of the prime minister, Anthony Eden, and marked the end of Britain's attempt to act as a world power. It occurred when Abdul Nasser, the Egyptian president, nationalised the Suez Canal. The canal was owned by the Suez Canal Company, in which Britain was a major shareholder.

Britain conspired with France and Israel to take over the canal and overthrow Nasser. Israeli troops invaded the Egyptian Sinai peninsula and British and French troops then occupied the Suez. However, Britain and France were forced into an embarrassing withdrawal because of opposition from the USA and the USSR.

4 *How successful was Heath as prime minister, 1970–74?*

4.1 THE ECONOMY

Government intervention

Edward Heath had taken over as Conservative leader from Alec Douglas Home and his successful 1970 election campaign had the Selsdon policy as its centre piece. This claimed that the Conservatives would not support ailing industries because they regarded the success or failure of companies as a natural condition of the economy. The policy began to collapse when Rolls-Royce Aero Engines faced bankruptcy in 1971 and the government intervened and provided the company with financial assistance. This was followed by a government backdown over the closure of Upper Clyde shipyards in Glasgow in 1972.

Economic management

The Heath government faced rising unemployment and the chancellor, Anthony Barber, became the last man to use Keynesian demand management techniques to reduce it. A 1972 increase in government spending led to the 'Barber boom' which reduced unemployment at the cost of stimulating inflation. The oil crisis of 1973 made inflation even worse.

4.2 INDUSTRIAL RELATIONS

The Industrial Relations Act, 1971

This Act was an attempt to control the power of the trade unions. It caused considerable resentment by forcing unions to submit industrial disputes to an industrial relations court. Many unions refused to comply.

The miners' strikes

In 1971–72, the National Union of Miners went on strike for higher wages and won. They organised a ban on overtime in 1973–74 and this resulted in Heath declaring a state of emergency and introducing a 3-day working week. In February 1974, Heath called an election on the issue and lost.

4.3 NORTHERN IRELAND

Internment, 1971

The introduction of internment without trial in 1971 caused great resentment among Irish nationalists and resulted in an increase in support for the IRA.

Bloody Sunday, 1972

The shooting of 14 civil rights demonstrators in Derry City led to the suspension of the Northern Ireland government and the introduction of direct rule from London.

The Sunningdale Agreement, 1973

In 1973, William Whitelaw, the secretary of state for Northern Ireland, negotiated the Sunningdale Agreement whereby the moderate Ulster Unionist Party under Brian Faulkner and the moderate nationalist SDLP joined a power-sharing executive.

4.4 BRITAIN JOINS THE EEC

In 1972, Britain signed the Treaty of Rome and at the beginning of 1973 joined the EEC along with Denmark and Ireland.

4.5 LOCAL GOVERNMENT

The Redcliffe-Maud Report on Local Government, 1972, recommended the creation of metropolitan counties in Merseyside, Manchester, West Midlands and Tyne and Wear. This was put into place in 1974 when the Conservatives also reorganised county government in England, Scotland and Wales.

4.6 UGANDA

In the 1972 Ugandan Asian crisis, the Ugandan president Idi Amin expelled thousands of Asians, the vast majority of whom came to live in Britain.

4.7 ELECTORAL DEFEAT

The Heath government went to the polls in February 1974 in order to gain electoral support to end a miners' ban on overtime which was causing an economic crisis. The election was marked by the rise of the Welsh and Scottish nationalist parties, and the Conservatives gained the most votes. The result had the Conservatives logging 11.8 million votes — 37.9% — compared with Labour's 37.1%. However, the Conservatives only won 297 seats to Labour's 301. Heath attempted to form a government with Liberal support and when this failed the Labour Party took office.

This topic appears at A2 in AQA Alternative U (Britain 1929–1997). Learn, understand and use historical terms associated with this topic such as 'Selsdon policy', 'industrial relations', 'internment' and 'power sharing'. At A2 you should use factual material to support and sustain an argument. You might be expected to explain whether or not Heath's administration was a success. You should try to produce a balanced analysis for and against his success.

5 How successful was Thatcher as prime minister, 1979–90?

5.1 MANAGEMENT OF THE ECONOMY

The Conservatives openly adopted monetarism and managed the economy through interest rates and control of the money supply. They also changed the burden of taxation by reducing direct income taxes and increasing indirect taxes such as VAT. State-owned industries were privatised — British Telecom, British Airways, British Gas and the electricity industry were floated on the stock market.

5.2 INDUSTRIAL RELATIONS

The Conservatives introduced legislation to control trade unions, including a ban on secondary picketing, a requirement for a secret ballot before a strike could be called and the confiscation of union funds when these conditions were not complied with. In 1984–85, the miners' strike was defeated by using these new powers, by drawing on a supply of coal stocks built up before the dispute and by deploying large numbers of police.

5.3 NORTHERN IRELAND
Hunger strikes

Jailed republican hunger strikers who demanded political status dominated Northern Irish politics in 1982–83. One hunger striker, Bobby Sands, was elected an MP in a by-election before he succeeded in starving himself to death.

The Anglo-Irish Agreement, 1985

The Anglo-Irish or Hillsborough Agreement was a turning point which recognised the Republic of Ireland's right to be consulted over Northern Ireland affairs. Meanwhile, the SAS was used to identify and assassinate active IRA members.

5.4 THE EEC
The Single European Act, 1985

Between 1979 and 1984, Margaret Thatcher negotiated a reduction in Britain's contribution to the EEC and, in 1985, she signed the Single European Act to create a single European market.

The Delors Report, 1989

The Delors Report recommended economic and monetary union, and Thatcher's growing opposition to increased EEC integration led to her downfall in 1990. The resignation of Geoffrey Howe, the deputy prime minister, sparked a leadership challenge from Michael Heseltine. Thatcher's inability to gain an outright victory on the first ballot led to her resignation.

5.5 FOREIGN POLICY

The Cold War

Thatcher was a fervent supporter of US President Reagan's strong stance against the USSR, and in 1983 she accepted the US deployment of Cruise missiles in Britain.

Rhodesia/Zimbabwe

The Lancaster House Agreement, 1979, ended war in Rhodesia and gave independence to Zimbabwe.

The Falklands War, 1982

When Argentine forces invaded the Falkland Islands, Thatcher organised the military expedition which retook them.

Hong Kong, 1984

The Hong Kong Agreement with China in 1984 confirmed that Britain would hand over its colony to communist China in 1997.

The Anglo-French Agreement, 1986

Under the terms of this agreement the French and British started work on building the Channel Tunnel.

EXAMINER'S TIP

This topic appears at A2 in AQA Alternative U (Britain 1929–1997). You should use information from this section to construct analytical answers. Questions could require you to assess the success of Thatcher's administration and might also ask you to assess whether she transformed Britain between 1979 and 1990.

---

6 | *How successful was Major as prime minister, 1990–97?*

6.1 ATTAINING POWER AND THE GULF WAR

John Major won the Conservative leadership election in a contest with Michael Heseltine and, in spite of an economic recession, was able to win the 1992 general election. Britain played a major part in the defeat of Iraq in Operation Desert Storm.

6.2 MANAGING THE ECONOMY

Conservatives continued to use monetarism and interest rates as major weapons to defeat inflation, and Chancellor Kenneth Clarke's control of the economy led to economic growth from 1994 to 1997. Major continued Thatcher's privatisation policy and sold off the water industry and the railways.

6.3 THE EXCHANGE RATE MECHANISM

As chancellor of the exchequer, Major had persuaded Thatcher to join the Exchange Rate Mechanism (ERM) in 1990. The aim was to create a stable pound by linking it to other European currencies, notably the German mark. By 1992, Britain was finding it increasingly difficult to keep its currency in line with the ERM requirement of £1 to DM2.95. When Britain suspended its membership of the ERM, the ensuing financial crisis almost brought down the government and Norman Lamont, Major's chancellor, was subsequently sacked.

6.4 NORTHERN IRELAND

In the 1993 Downing Street Agreement with the Irish Republic, Britain announced that it had no selfish economic or strategic interest in Northern Ireland. An IRA cease-fire in 1994–96 followed the Downing Street Declaration but ended when no political progress was made.

6.5 THE EEC AND CONSERVATIVE SPLITS

Britain signed the 1992 Maastricht Treaty which created the European Union, but Britain refused to accept the *Social Chapter*. The treaty was narrowly accepted by the House of Commons.

Conservative splits over Europe

In 1995, continual criticism from the right wing led Major to resign as Conservative leader and seek re-election. He then defeated the Eurosceptic John Redwood.

6.6 POLITICAL SLEAZE AND ELECTORAL DEFEAT

The Conservatives were soundly defeated in the 1997 general election. (See the end of Unit 16 on the Labour Party 1945–97 for broad reasons for the Conservatives' electoral defeat.) Sleaze was a major issue in the campaign with scandals such as:
- the Scott Inquiry into arms to Iraq, 1992
- the Nolan Committee into Standards in Public Life, 1994
- Neil Hamilton and cash for questions, 1994–97

GLOSSARY

Social Chapter: part of the Maastricht Treaty covering workers' rights.

EXAMINER'S TIP

This topic appears at A2 in AQA Alternative U (Britain 1929–1997). You may be expected to assess Major's policies and decide whether, on balance, they were a success or failure. You may also be asked to explain why the Conservatives lost so badly in the 1997 election. If so, place and explain the reasons in order of importance. Try to identify links between reasons.